Body Languag

A play

Alan Ayckbourn

Samuel French — London
New York - Toronto - Hollywood

BODY LANGUAGE

First presented at the Stephen Joseph Theatre in the Round, Scarborough, on 21st May 1990 with the following cast of characters:

Hravic Zyergefoovc	Nigel Anthony
Freya Roope	Cecily Hobbs
Benjamin Cooper	Geoffrey Whitehead
Ronnie Weston	Timothy Kightley
Angie Dell	Lia Williams
Derek Short	Peter Forbes
Jo Knapton	Tam Hoskyns
Mal Bennet	Robert McCulley

Directed by **Alan Ayckbourn**
Designed by **Roger Glossop**
Lighting by **Mick Hughes**
Music by **John Pattison**

CHARACTERS

Hravic Zyergefoovc, a surgeon, 84
Freya Roope, a nurse, 40
Benjamin Cooper, a surgeon, 50
Ronnie Weston, an agent, 41
Angie Dell, a model, 30
Derek Short, a photographer, 34
Jo Knapton, a reporter, 30
Mal Bennet, a bass player, 50
Extras: **nurses**

The action of the play takes place in the Othman Clinic, somewhere in the south of rural England

Time—June to October, recently

Act I
 Scene 1 A morning in June
 Scene 2 Some weeks later

Act II
 Scene 1 Two days later. Morning
 Scene 2 A few days later. Morning
 Scene 3 A few days later. Evening
 Scene 4 Later. Morning

ACT I

Scene I

A sunny June morning at the Othman Clinic, somewhere in the south of rural England

Originally a splendid Georgian country home, this expensive and magnificently appointed clinic set in its own grounds deals exclusively with the very rich, and specialises in discreet cosmetic surgery

Our view is of a part of the rear terrace. Several of the most expensive rooms have their own doors opening directly on to this. Presumably so that on fine days like today the more fortunate patients may sit outside to recuperate

We also have a partial view of two such rooms—but not very much of them. A small writing table perhaps, near the window. A chair. No sight of a bed or a patient. From time to time, we might catch sight of a doctor or a nurse, even a visitor, and if any of these speak we shall hear them. But anyone out of sight, we won't hear. Thus we're likely to overhear a number of one-sided conversations. All these areas, the terrace and the rooms, are raised. From the terrace there are stone steps that lead down to the garden path and the lawns beyond. We get a suggestion of this as well. Alongside the steps a wooden ramp has been added to accommodate wheelchairs

At the start, the stage is empty. The birds sing. The sun shines

After a moment, Hravic enters from the garden. He wears battered comfortable clothes and a panama hat. He is old, physically frail and walks slowly and with difficulty with the aid of two sticks. Mentally, though, he is very alert and very little escapes him. He enjoys the privilege that old age has given him to be outrageous, cantankerous and frequently downright offensive—especially to women. Fortunately, he speaks hardly a word of English so we are often left to guess the gist of his remarks (unless they're translated for us). Just what his origins are is never specified. Probably, but not certainly, Eastern European. At any rate, to assist pronunciation, his language will be written here phonetically whenever possible, together with an accompanying literal translation in square brackets

Hravic slowly makes his way to the foot of the steps

Hravic (*muttering to himself, irritably*) Droot ... drooten stucks! Oook! Oook! Een karnet ruudst hriet sairer groat! Sairer groat een karnet browled. Darnt ip broont im sairer groat limp trotter. [Sod it! Sodding sticks! Ow! Ow! Twenty years ago I could have run this distance. Twenty years ago I would have sprinted it. Now it takes me nearly twenty years just to cross a lawn.] (*He calls*) Freya! Freya! (*Muttering*) Vess putt, Memmer Hrootpucker. (*Yelling*) Freya! Har spruntgutt. Hoot! Hoot! Bowelstain! [Freya! Freya! (*Muttering*) Where's she got to, Madame Dyke? (*Yelling*) Freya! You useless pudding. Here! Here! Bear's dropping!]

Freya comes from the garden. She is carrying a rug and some other bits and pieces of Hravic's paraphernalia—notebooks, writing materials, etc. She is probably in her mid-forties. It's hard to tell. She could be younger; or she might be much older. Whilst not dressed in uniform, Freya manages to make the plain, simple summer clothes she does wear seem almost like one. Her manner is impassive and her expression inscrutable. The stream of abuse that Hravic directs at her has apparently no effect whatsoever. She treats him and his varying moods with a mixture of nurse to patient, secretary to boss, niece to elderly uncle, or occasionally something closer than that

Freya Vruyt! Vruyt! Nord kinst vin grengels sanglevellerkiss. [Wait! Wait! I can't be in two places at once.]
Hravic (*grumpily*) Nord een quester har vin grengels. Zim grengel butter. Vess een'st. Gool brutt questicer loo gobble? [I'm not asking you to be in two places. One place, that's all. Where I am. Is that too much to ask?]
Freya (*ignoring this tirade*) Fenk har hrissich borric grerb? [Do you want to go inside, now?]
Hravic (*grumpily*) Noot. Ip gool loo zooty. Een fiss ticker. [No. It's too nice. I want to walk.]
Freya Lololo. Butter gitts nord sild. [All right. Only don't get tired.]
Hravic Sild? Een ribbiss goop ackerdengloos zan har rult, Memmer Hrootpucker. [Tired? I still have more energy than you, Madame Dyke.]
Freya (*through gritted teeth*) Nord een'st hrootpucker, een tottst indivard. [I am not a dyke, I keep telling you.]
Hravic (*evilly*) Een ribbist harg zoop far brutt, wickins. [I have only your word for that, dearest.] (*Leering*) Vessderck cricklestick? [Fancy a screw?]
Freya Har gult ut peeker offle fild. [You are an evil old man.]

Hravic finds this exchange very amusing. He laughs a lot. Freya remains impassive

At this point, Benjamin appears in one of the rooms. He is a well groomed, smartly dressed man of fifty. Although he evidently takes great care with his appearance and probably cuts quite a dash with his female patients, he makes no attempt at concealing his age, no attempt to "youthen" himself. He looks and behaves his age. He enters backwards, evidently conversing with a patient whom we can't see or hear

Hravic and Freya watch from the garden and, as they see Benjamin, have an exchange overlapping the end of his speech

Benjamin (*to the invisible patient*) ...No, no. That's perfectly in order. There's nothing to stop you doing that, Mrs Bartholemew. I'll leave you with nurse, then... I'll see you before you leave, yes...
Hravic (*under the last*) Ah! Hoor Benjamin gool. [Ah! There's Benjamin.]
Freya Jit. Hoor Metter Cooper gool. [Yes. There's Mr Cooper.]

Benjamin sees Hravic and goes to greet him

Benjamin Ah, Hravic, my dear friend. Good morning! Hroos dinker!
Hravic (*expansively*) Benjamin! Hroos dinker!
Benjamin (*warmly, to Freya*) Hroos dinker, Freya!
Freya Good morning, Mr Cooper!
Benjamin No, no, no. Now, I told you last night, please, Benjamin.
Freya Benjamin.
Hravic (*embracing Benjamin and kissing him on both cheeks*) Ah! Hroos dinker, imst offle, offle trooch. [Good morning, my old, old friend.]
Benjamin (*rather embarrassed by this show of affection*) Hroos dinker!
Hravic Good morning, olt friend.
Benjamin Good morning. Yes...
Hravic Gobo! Gobo! [Hallo! Hallo!]
Benjamin Gobo!
Hravic Hallo. Good day. God bless. Scrawn bat! [Long life!]
Benjamin (*quite moved by all this*) Scrawn bat! Scrawn bat, indeed! Yes. And we have beautiful weather to welcome you both here on your first morning.

Hravic looks puzzled. Freya, who has watched this display without comment, now swiftly translates as she does throughout

Freya Zooty critt, harg zimter dinker.
Hravic Yit! Yit! Benshtergeel. Benshtergeel. Harg hroops. Stint.
Freya (*to Benjamin*) He says beautiful! And your gardens are stunning.
Benjamin Benshtergeel. Yes, I remember now, that means beautiful, doesn't it?

Hravic Benshtergeel, Benjamin, olt friend.

Freya You remember some words?

Benjamin No, alas, no. I used to speak fairly fluently but that was thirty years ago. Gone now, I'm afraid. Har rult ollies benshtergeel... You have beautiful eyes. I remember that...

Freya Olbiss. Olbiss are eyes... Not ollies.

Benjamin Oh, olbiss.

Freya (*solemnly*) Not ollies. Ollies are shoulder blades. Har ruit olbiss benshtergeel.

Benjamin Ah. No wonder the girls looked at me rather strangely...

Freya (*to Hravic*) Ip dilt, har ruit ollies benshtergeel.

Hravic (*laughing*) Ollies benshtergeeel. Brutt hroos! [That's good!]

Freya Ip tult olbiss. [He meant eyes.]

Hravic Jit olbiss. Olbiss.

Benjamin (*enjoying this rather extended joke*) Yes.

Hravic Har sic bootch umper ollies, Freya. Een fiss gitter imst putt im brotten. (*He laughs*) [You should have a look at Freya's shoulder blades, sometime. I'd like to get my hands on those.]

Benjamin (*laughing too*) What did he say?

Freya (*frowning*) Not possible to translate.

Benjamin You've had breakfast, I hope?

Freya Oh, yes. We're just taking a little stroll.

Benjamin Good. Good. I have to finish my morning round. Then I'll join you for some coffee.

Freya Good.

Benjamin Er... Will you remind Hravic that we did agree he agreed to talk to this radio journalist this morning. This interviewer. He agreed to do just the one. If he remembers...

Freya Oh, yes. He remembers. Britt tokenstrappel. Har prigrool? [This journalist. You remember?]

Hravic Oh, lololo, jit. Een prigst. [Oh, all right, yes. I remember.]

Freya No difficult questions, though, please.

Benjamin No, there'll be no difficult questions. I've explained that quite clearly to them. It's just local radio, nothing very important. But they've been very helpful to us here at the clinic in the past and... Well, they'll be here in about half an hour's time. Is that all right?

Freya Yes. We will continue strolling.

Benjamin (*beaming at her*) Splendid. See you in a minute, then. Zutter donk, offle trooch. [Until then, old friend.]

Hravic Ah, Benjamin, my friend. Zutter donk! (*He embraces Benjamin again. As he does so, he spells it out*) Int gobble rain on harg panter. Eh? Eh? [And much lead in your pencil.]

Benjamin (*puzzled, to Freya*) I'm sorry, what's he saying?

Freya (*frowning*) Not possible to translate. (*To Hravic, starting to lead him off along the garden*) Bim! Bim in, har rally spalchoffle. [Come! Come on.]

Hravic (*as they go*) Povleek! Tinny hrootpucker. [Lead on! Little dyke.]

Freya (*grimly*) Nord een'st hrootpucker. [I am not a dyke.]

Benjamin watches them as Hravic and Freya go off up the garden

Benjamin (*gazing after them*) Yes. (*He enjoys the sunshine for a second*)

A nurse appears briefly in Mrs Bartholemew's room, folding a blanket. She soon goes but the movement is sufficient to bring Benjamin back to the present

Ah, well. Ever onward. (*He turns and is about to enter the other room*)

Ronnie, a sharply dressed man of about forty, appears in the doorway

Ronnie Good morning, doctor.

Benjamin Ah, Mr... Good morning...

Ronnie Ronnie Weston. Angie's personal manager. I accompanied Angie down here yesterday, if you recall?

Benjamin Yes, indeed I do. Have you come from London? You must have started out very early.

Ronnie Oh, no. I stayed over.

Benjamin Stayed over?

Ronnie Locally. In the village. Frankly, I didn't go back to London last night. I wanted to stay close to her, you see. Close to Angie. She's valuable, she's special, she's a unique property and she needs someone to watch over her. You know what I mean?

Benjamin (*vaguely*) Oh, well, that's...

Ronnie So I stayed at the *Fox and Hat*...

Benjamin *Hounds*. Yes. I believe it's quite pleasant there. One or two relatives of patients have... How did you find it?

Ronnie Unspeakable.

Benjamin Really?

Ronnie Beyond description.

Benjamin Well, of course, we are in the country...

Ronnie My friend, we are in the Antarctica, believe me, the *Fox and Hat* is the Dhobi Desert of catering. No lower could you sink, anywhere, believe me, not even if you were drowning. Now, doctor, I know you're a busy man——

Benjamin Mister.

Ronnie I know you're a busy man … sorry?

Benjamin Not doctor. Just Mister.

Ronnie (*puzzled*) Mister?

Benjamin I'm a surgeon. Not a doctor. Mister.

Ronnie Oh, right. Mister it shall be. Well, I just wanted to ask you about Angie, you see. How is she? Between us? Was it all satisfactory, Mister?

Benjamin Oh, yes, quite in order. I was actually just on my way to see how she——

Ronnie I mean, tell me, Mister, is she fit enough to get up yet? Your honest opinion.

Benjamin Well…

Ronnie Only every second she's flat on her back—well, in a career like hers, my time is money, if you understand me, Mister. I mean, frankly I'd like her upright as soon as is humanely possible without risk to her health and strength, of course…

Benjamin Oh, yes, yes, indeed. I'm sure she could be—upright—fairly soon, really. But any operation, however minor…

Ronnie Yes…

Benjamin …however routine…

Ronnie …yes, yes…

Benjamin …is still an operation, you understand…?

Ronnie …yes, yes, yes…

Benjamin …Can still be fairly traumatic to the system, even a young and healthy one like hers…

Ronnie Oh, she's a fit girl, Mister. She's supremely fit.

Benjamin …needs a few hours at least to recover…

Ronnie Angie has a body like a well-honed bow string…

Benjamin …and to recuperate, of course.

Ronnie The care that girl takes of her body. The care. Endless. I tell you, it puts yours and mine to shame.

Benjamin Oh, yes.

Ronnie I tell people she's not a model, she's an athlete. She's a pedigree racehorse.

Benjamin Yes, yes…

Ronnie So I can take her home this evening? Would that be in order? Give her a good night's sleep so she can be up and about for a session first thing tomorrow morning, is that the picture you're giving me?

Benjamin Now, now, we really do have to ask the patient herself. We'll see how she feels at, say, lunchtime. In fact, you must let me see her now, Mr Weston.

Ronnie Yes, of course… I'll be ruled by you, Mister.

Benjamin I'll let you have my opinion, once I've…

Ronnie Only—normally I would never ask this—tomorrow is something I would not want to see cancelled for her. It's top secret. All I can tell you is, it is prestigious, it is underwear and it is very, very big. Enough said?

Benjamin As I say, we'll have to see how...

Angie appears in her room and comes to the doorway. She has on her dressing gown over her night things. She looks rather pale and unmade-up, but, despite this, still manages to look stunning. A pretty rather than beautiful face atop a body that, from what we can discern, almost lives up to Ronnie's description of it

Angie (*sleepily*) What a lovely day, innit?

Benjamin (*mildly alarmed*) Ah, now, Miss Dell—I don't think you should be doing that quite so soon...

Angie Oh, hallo. Pardon?

Benjamin Walking about. You should be resting, you know.

Angie No, I feel great. Honestly. I hate lying in bed for long. I get restless.

Ronnie (*to Benjamin, confidentially*) Fit, you see? Fit.

Angie Look at these gardens, they're amazing. Are they all yours, then?

Benjamin Yes. They belong to the clinic, yes. Look, why don't you have a seat out here? I'll get nurse to bring you a rug. And a cushion.

Angie Yes, all right. Fabulous.

Ronnie Go on, sit down, Angie. Do what Mister says.

Angie (*mildly irritated*) I'm going to, I just said.

Ronnie (*indicating a chair*) Come on ... sit over here.

Angie I am, I am...

Benjamin That's very hard that chair. She'll need a cushion.

Ronnie I'll get a cushion, it's all right, I'll fetch one. No need to disturb the nurses. Busy people. Angie, you wait there with Mister.

Benjamin (*tiring of this mode of address*) Benjamin, please.

Ronnie Sorry?

Benjamin Just call me Benjamin. It's much simpler.

Ronnie Right you are. In that case, Ronnie, please. And this is Angie, of course. Just a second.

Ronnie hurries off into Angie's room

Angie That's a nice name, Benjamin. I like that name.

Benjamin Oh, thank you.

Angie You get called Ben a lot then, do you? Do people tend to call you Ben?

Benjamin Er, no. No, hardly anyone at all, really.

Angie What do they call you, then?

Benjamin Well, Benjamin. Or Mr Cooper.

Angie Mr Cooper?

Benjamin Yes—it tends to happen when one's a surgeon.
Angie Oh, I see.
Benjamin But... (*He gesticulates vaguely*)
Angie You don't mind me calling you Benjamin, do you?
Benjamin No. Please.
Angie Ben?
Benjamin Benjamin.
Angie Benjamin. (*She smiles at him*)

Angie is not a vamp or a seductress. Hers is the smile of the girl next door, sincere and spontaneous. It's a smile that has made her and those around her a lot of money. It now captivates Benjamin

Benjamin (*collecting himself*) Well, now, how's the ... how are those stitches? Are they comfortable? I take it they've been—you've been looked at this morning.
Angie Oh, yes.

A pause. She smiles at him again. Benjamin smiles back

Did you want to have a look, then, do you?
Benjamin A look at what?
Angie At my stitches? I mean, were you waiting to examine them?
Benjamin No, no, no, no.

Slight pause

No, no. I don't want to disturb the dressing. They're comfortable?
Angie Oh, yes.
Benjamin Good.
Angie A bit itchy.
Benjamin Ah, well. That's inevitable. You shouldn't have any problems, the—area all round the upper leg, it's very resilient, very quick to heal. Usually.
Angie It's not my leg, is it?
Benjamin No, no.
Angie It's my bum.
Benjamin Yes, yes. Absolutely right. Yes.
Angie (*amused*) That's why I'm waiting for a cushion. I hope you knew which bit of me was which when you were operating?
Benjamin Oh, yes, you bet. Have no fear of that. But, you know, when you see as many bodies as we do... A surgeon friend of mine used to say, a horizontal body he always treated clinically, dispassionately and

professionally; vertical ones, he felt at liberty to treat as he liked. (*He laughs*) That is with certain horizontal exceptions, of course.

Angie (*laughing*) Unless he always had it standing up.

Benjamin (*laughing out of control now*) Oh, no, no. Even surgeons have to lie down occasionally, you know...

Angie (*laughing*) I should hope so...

Eventually they both stop laughing

How did we get on to that, then?

Benjamin I—I've no idea.

Angie I expect you're always getting on to that, aren't you? In your line?

Benjamin No, no... Not that frequently, no. Actually we tend to try and avoid it. Normally.

Angie Oh. (*Wondering if he might be gay*) Are you married, then?

Benjamin No. Divorced.

Angie Oh.

Benjamin Well. (*He gesticulates again*)

Angie I wish I was.

Benjamin Married?

Angie Divorced.

Benjamin Ah. You're married?

Angie Yes. You knew that, didn't you? Surely?

Benjamin Yes, I believe I did read...

Angie You couldn't miss it. (*Suddenly sharp*) Everyone in the whole bloody world knows about that marriage...

Pause

(*Softening*) Sorry.

Benjamin No.

A grim-faced nurse enters, carrying a rug and a cushion. She is followed by a rather apologetic Ronnie

During the following, the nurse places the cushion on one of the chairs

Ronnie Here we are. Here we are, then.

The nurse grimly indicates for Angie to sit in the chair. Angie does so obediently. The nurse then tucks the rug briskly around her, leaving Angie somewhat cocooned

(*As this proceeds*) I'm afraid I rather upset this good lady just now by trying to help myself to some cushions from the lounge. I didn't realize you kept special cushions. So I'm afraid I'm rather in her bad books. (*To nurse*) That's lovely, nurse. A beautiful job of work. God bless you.

The nurse's expression doesn't change. She starts to leave, back through Angie's room

Angie Ta.
Benjamin Thank you, nurse.

The nurse goes

They can get—proprietorial about certain areas. One just has to learn to tread tactfully.
Ronnie I thought we might give them all a little something when we leave. A couple of crates of champagne perhaps for the nurses...
Benjamin Oh, good heavens...
Ronnie Vintage Bollinger. A case of scotch for the doctors...
Benjamin No, no, really. That's not at all necessary.
Angie Come on, Ronnie, what's the point of getting them all pissed, they're operating on people...
Ronnie Just a token, that's all...
Angie Then give them some sweets...
Benjamin Sweets. Yes, a splendid idea.
Ronnie Chocolates.
Benjamin Chocolates ... perfect.
Ronnie A big box of chocolates, then. A twenty pound box? Circular. I know where I can get one of those.
Angie (*fiercely*) Ronnie, all they want is an ordinary pissing box of Dairy Milk, that's all!
Ronnie All right! All right!
Angie (*muttering*) Pillock! He always has to buy size twenty.

Slight pause. Angie smiles at Benjamin

I hate chocolate.
Benjamin (*a little embarrassed*) Well, I think I must be moving along... See you a little later, probably.
Angie Yes. (*She smiles*) Bye bye.
Ronnie (*confidentially drawing Benjamin aside*) Er, Ben, there's still been no ... press enquiries, have there? Media interest over all this with Angie...
Benjamin Oh, you mean...? (*He indicates Angie*) No.
Ronnie No unusual phone calls? No strangers prowling about?

Benjamin Oh, no...

Ronnie Reasonably discreet, your people, I trust...

Benjamin Yes, as I say, they're quite used to celebrities here.

Ronnie I mean, if the lowbrow press got wind Angie was here, they'd be hanging off your gutter work... You know what I mean?

Benjamin No-one has breathed a word. I promise you.

Angie and Benjamin exchange one more smile

Benjamin leaves

Ronnie You rest there till lunchtime, I'm going to make a few phone calls.

Angie Fetch me my sun-glasses, will you?

Ronnie I'll get the car here for three o'clock. Gentle drive back to the flat. Early night and then first thing tomorrow we're down to Bournemouth, OK?

Angie They're just on the table in there.

Ronnie You got that?

Angie Yes. Sun-glasses.

Ronnie moves into the room and gets her glasses from the desk

Ronnie (*as he does*) I hope you're taking all this in, Ange. It's an important session tomorrow. I want you fresh, I want you looking good.

Angie (*irritably*) All right...

Ronnie (*handing her the sun-glasses*) Here.

Angie Put them on for me, will you?

Ronnie What's the matter with you? You haven't had your arms removed, have you?

Angie I'm recuperating from surgery, I'd like a little consideration for once.

Ronnie Surgery. You had a mole cut off your backside, that's all...

Angie It was not a mole. It was a non-malignant growth. And it bloody hurt.

Ronnie (*putting on her glasses*) Here.

Angie Careful, that's my eye!

Ronnie I'm going to phone.

Angie And it's staying covered up tomorrow because it's still got stitches in, all right?

Ronnie It's not nude. It's underwear. You'll be covered.

Angie Underwear?

Ronnie Yes.

Angie In Bournemouth?

Ronnie Yes. They wanted seaside.

Angie It's not rubber again, is it?

Ronnie No, no, no.

Angie I'm not doing any more of that.

Ronnie You're beyond all that...

Angie That brought them all out of the woodwork. I had kinky letters for weeks. And a rash and all.

Ronnie Listen, Angie, one more time, right? Take all the work you can, girl, while you can. Because tomorrow it may not be——

Angie (*with him*) ...it may not be there...

Ronnie Right. As of now, you are in demand, you are at your peak, the world is at your oyster. But you are thirty years old, girl...

Angie Yes, thank you...

Ronnie Somewhere out there is a kid of eighteen waiting to grab your chair the minute you look like you're sliding under the table...

Angie I've got other plans, haven't I?

Ronnie Yes, I know you do. But those are still plans, Angie. At the planning stage. This is real. This is now. This is tangible assets. I'm talking tangible, not notional.

Angie Not only notional. That film contract from Deacon, that's a bloody sight more than notional, isn't it?

Ronnie Not signed. Nothing is signed, Angie. It's notional. When it's signed, I'll be the first to break open the Dom Perrier, I promise you...

Angie And there's the record...

Ronnie Not signed. Angie, that record is a twinkle in Ralph's eye. It's not even a gleam, Angie, let alone a mote. It's a little teeny twinkle. I've told you, the man's bad news. You'd have to open a damn sight more than your mouth to get a singing contract out of him...

Angie (*despairingly*) Oh God, Ronnie, leave it out. Don't jump on everything, will you...?

Ronnie I'm not jumping on them, I'm merely being... (*He stops suddenly and stares out into the garden*) Hallo. What's that?

Angie What?

Ronnie I thought I saw someone in the bushes down there.

Angie Who?

Ronnie I don't know. (*He stares*) I'll be happier when I get you away from here. That mob gets wind... Angie Dell in a clinic. They'll make hay with that.

Angie There's only one person worries me and that's my husband.

Ronnie Mal? He doesn't know.

Angie He may find out. He's obsessive. I tell you.

Ronnie He's had the second court order. He has to keep away. He wouldn't dare.

Angie When's that ever stopped him? He's mad. I married a lunatic. Any other man you say go away, they go away. Eventually. They get the

message. Mal, he's crazy. He's taken so much stuff his brain's exploded.
I tell you, Ronnie, he frightens me. I don't get frightened easily but Mal
sometimes scares the shit out of me…

Ronnie As soon as we get back I'll have him sorted out. I'll have him seen
to.

Angie (*sarcastically*) Seen to? What are you going to do, then, knock him
off?

Ronnie No. But I can find people who'll give him a—firm talking to.

Angie Terrific. The last time I hit him in the face with a lighted standard lamp.
That didn't discourage him, did it?

Ronnie Well, these lads can be—fairly persuasive. Beaky uses them.

Angie Beaky Dawson?

Ronnie Occasionally.

Angie Bloody hell.

Ronnie So.

Angie I don't want to be a widow, you know.

Ronnie (*starting to leave*) See you in a minute.

Angie I'm not having nothing more to do with men. I've finished with them.
(*After him*) Especially you!

Ronnie has gone

(*Muttering*) Berk! And I'm not getting involved with Beaky Dawson,
either. Finish up part of a flyover. (*She wriggles*) Bloody woman's
wrapped me up like a chrysalis. (*She winces*) Ah! I've been kicked in the
bum by a horse. Oooh! Ow! Ooo!

*As Angie writhes about in her chair trying to get comfortable, Derek
appears on the lawn. He is in his thirties, casually dressed in anorak and
jeans. Slung about him is the minimal paraphernalia of the professional
"paparazzi" photographer*

*He watches Angie amused. He raises his camera and fires off one or two
frames with his motor drive. Angie freezes at the sound, like a gundog*

Oh, God!

Derek (*grinning*) Hallo, Angie. What are you doing hiding from us, naughty
girl?

Angie Piss off.

Derek Just a couple.

Angie Off piss.

Derek Two pictures. Just two.

Angie I warn you, I'll yell for someone. I'll have you chucked out.

Derek One picture.

Angie One? When have you ever taken one?

Derek One. Promise.

Angie With that thing. What are you talking about? You've already taken forty.

Derek (*pleading*) Angie!

Angie Where are the rest of you buggers, then? Where are they all hiding? Bottom of the pond?

Derek Just me, Ange. Promise.

Angie How did you get on to us, anyway?

Derek Secret source.

Angie Someone from Ronnie's office? It's that secretary of his, isn't it? Myrtle, whatever her name is.

Derek No, it wasn't Moira. Come on, Angie. Couple of shots, I'm gone. Promise.

Angie Not till you tell me who.

Derek This used to be my patch. I used to work down here.

Angie What, in this place? There's only five cows and a sheep.

Derek We've all got to start somewhere. It was a local tip-off. That's all I'm saying.

Angie Derek Short, the country boy. Explains a lot.

Derek Local paper. Weddings, funerals and cattle shows.

Angie Business as usual, then. Go on, piss off.

Derek Angie... If I go now, what's to say in less than an hour there won't be dozens of us swarming around?

Angie You berk.

Derek You going to tell them all to go away?

Angie You prick.

Derek Whereas, at the moment, it's just little me with one little camera.

Angie You're a real shit, aren't you?

Derek Oh, come on, come on, Angie... Don't make it personal. It's professional.

Angie (*getting up*) All right, what do you want, then? Close ups of my stitches? That do you?

Derek Oh, come on... What do you think I am?

Angie I'm running out of words. I'll put my tweed suit on then, shall I?

Derek Are you wearing a bandage? I could use a shot of the bandage...

Angie No, you won't. You'll get one sitting, one standing and that's it. No tits, no bums, no bandages. I'm a bloody invalid, you pillock.

Derek Bless you, Angie, bless you. You're a lady.

Angie And you can wait till I've put my face on and all. I don't want any like this, understood?

Derek Fair enough, Angie. I mean, honestly, don't blame me. Blame the public, darling. They're the ones who are interested. They want to know about you, they're fascinated by you. They love you...

Angie Oh, spare me that, Derek. I'm not straight out of school... (*She moves to her room*)

Derek God bless you, darling. Quick as you can.

Angie (*muttering as she goes into her room*) Honestly, a person can't even die in peace these days...

Angie goes off

Derek, greatly cheered, whistles to himself. He raises his camera speculatively and points it into the room after her

Angie returns like a shot

You dare. You just dare. I promise you, you will never look down a lens again because I will stick both your eyes out with my nail scissors, all right? If you think I'm joking, try me. I mean it.

Derek I believe you, Angie.

Angie You better had, Derek.

Angie goes again

Derek toys with the idea of a shot but decides maybe she isn't joking. He wanders along the terrace, looking in windows, hopefully. He goes down the steps and on to the lawn, stepping back as he does so, as if to get in a shot of the whole house

Derek disappears from view

After a moment, Benjamin appears in the other room

He turns and speaks to someone we can't immediately see

Benjamin ...Yes, I think it's quicker to pop through this way. This room's temporarily unoccupied. This way.

Jo appears. Like Angie, a woman who's just reached thirty. But she is at least, physically, everything Angie isn't. Of similar basic build and height, Jo has let herself go. She is greatly overweight and makes little effort with her appearance. Her hair is a mess, her face red and puffy from unhealthy living, her nails are badly bitten. She is a woman in crisis, at odds with herself. She carries a large shoulder bag and a portable tape recorder

I suggest you might like to do the interview out here. It's fairly quiet, you shouldn't be disturbed—(*he sees Angie's empty chair*) oh, yes, good, she's gone back inside—unless the birds and so on upset your tape recorder, I don't know...

Jo No, this is fine. This'll be fine.

Benjamin I'll try and locate Professor Zyergefoovc. They said they were going for a stroll...

Jo Is that how to pronounce it? Zyergef...

Benjamin Zyergefoovc. Zy—er—ge—foovc...

Jo (*trying it*) Zyergefoovc...

Benjamin No, more—foovc—push your mouth forward more ... foovc...

Jo ...foovc...

Benjamin That's it ... foovc...

Jo ...foovc...

Benjamin That's it. Very good.

Jo Zyergefoovc.

Benjamin Excellent. Professor Hravic Zyergefoovc.

Jo I think I'll just call him by his surname.

Benjamin Well, that might be sensible. By the way, a word of warning. Hravic's English is less good than I thought. As I explained, we haven't met for thirty years, merely corresponded and I'm afraid in that time, isolated as he has been from the West, he's forgotten most of what he knew...

Jo (*alarmed*) He doesn't speak English at all?

Benjamin Very—very sparingly. He does have an excellent interpreter, Freya Roope. I'm afraid it'll have to be conducted mostly through her.

Jo (*very perturbed*) Oh, God...

Benjamin Is that a problem for you?

Jo Of course it's a problem. I'm supposed to be doing a radio interview. Oh, this is absurd. Why didn't they tell me? Why didn't anyone tell me?

Benjamin (*looking at her rather apprehensively*) I hope you were warned, there's to be nothing controversial. Those were the terms for this interview.

Jo He's not going to object to discussing his work, surely?

Benjamin No, but only in general terms, please.

Jo I mean, that's really all there is of interest, isn't there? His work?

Benjamin All I'm saying is, he's over eighty years old, he's pioneered some of the most extraordinary surgical techniques in the history of medicine, and we don't want to have him side-tracked into the more sensational aspects of his work.

Jo You don't deny that he's been involved in one or two rather dubious procedures? Ethically dubious?

Benjamin Dubious to us in this country, possibly. But he is from a part of the world where certain practices are less frowned upon...

Jo That doesn't make them any more ethical, surely?

Benjamin No, no, no... Now, listen, Miss Knapton, I do have to put my foot down very firmly here. Hravic is here on a purely private visit. The only reason your radio station has been granted this exclusive interview is because of your help and co-operation in the past. But if you intend to pursue that line of questioning, you'd better leave now.

A slight pause

Jo (*reluctantly*) We can discuss the weather, I suppose.

Benjamin You'd rather not proceed?

Jo No, I—won't pursue that line of questioning. I promise.

Benjamin Splendid. Thank you. I'm sure there's still lots you'll find to talk about. I'm sure there is.

Jo (*drily*) I'll think of something.

Benjamin I'll find them for you. I think they were walking somewhere.

Benjamin goes

Jo starts to unpack her gear

In a moment, Derek wanders back into view

He glances at Jo disinterestedly

(*Nodding to Jo, casually*) Morning. Lovely day.

Jo Hallo, Derek.

Derek (*staring at her for a second, incredulously*) My God! Jo Knapton.

Jo Derek Short.

Derek Eight years?

Jo Something like that.

Derek How are you, then?

Jo Fine.

Derek You've—altered. I didn't——

Jo (*curtly*) You haven't. Busy?

Derek Earning a crumb, you know...

Jo I see quite a bit of your stuff these days.

Derek Oh, well, right place, right time. Luck of the game.

Jo Really? You used to tell me you made your own luck, I seem to remember.

Derek What about you? Still with the old *Advertiser*?

Jo No. I left two years ago. Got taken over, didn't you know? I couldn't stick it another minute. I'm with local radio.

Derek You should have done that years ago. I was always telling you to get out.

Jo Yes, but you were telling me for quite different reasons, Derek.

Derek So you'd get on...

Jo Not at all. So you'd get on. So I could chuck it all in and trail after you.

Derek You underestimate yourself. You always have done. You've got talent. Masses of it.

Jo Thank you.

Derek I mean it. You shouldn't be wasting it.

Jo I'm not wasting it.

Derek You should be using it.

Jo I am using it.

Derek Seriously. Stuck away down here with a tape recorder.

Jo I like it down here.

Derek Here?

Jo Yes.

Derek Jesus.

Jo If it's all that terrible what are you doing, then?

Derek (*evasively*) Well...

Jo A series on architecture, is it? For one of the Sundays? A pull-out guide to plastic surgeons?

Derek I think I'm here for the same reason you are, quite probably.

Jo (*alarmed*) Really?

Derek I suspect so.

Jo Listen, Derek. I have the exclusive here.

Derek Oh, come on...

Jo I was granted this interview on the understanding that I would be the only person——

Derek (*shouting her down*) Listen, listen, don't start shouting exclusive, not to me, darling——

Jo (*talking over him*) Would you let me finish? That I would be the only person he would be prepared——

Derek ——first come, first served, that's the way these things work and as far as I'm concerned I was here first, I have been standing here for nearly an hour. She has agreed to pose, she is happy for me to take pictures and I intend to take pictures and then leave, all right? Once I've done that, you can talk to her to your heart's content. You can put her out with the farming news, I don't care.

Jo Her?

Derek I don't know why you want her on radio. Like broadcasting a juggling panda, isn't it?

Jo Who are we talking about?

Derek Who are you talking about?

Jo Not the same person as you.

Derek Is there somebody else here?

Jo (*evasively*) Possibly.

Derek Well, come on? Who?

Jo You tell yours first.

Derek Tell me yours, I'll tell you mine.

Jo Yours first.

Derek (*after a slight hesitation*) Angie Dell.

Jo Who?

Derek Angie Dell.

Jo What, her...?

Derek Sssh! Eric tipped me off she was here.

Jo Eric Whitton?

Derek Yes, we still have a drink together occasionally.

Jo Just the one?

Derek Apparently his sister-in-law's niece is a cleaner here and she got the word that Angie Dell was booked in for minor surgery...

Jo To have her brain put back...

Derek So. There you are.

Jo Well, thank you, Derek, I really can't wait to interview her. I'll do my best to get her economic forecasts in time for the one o'clock news.

Derek Not interested, I take it?

Jo I'd sooner talk to a sheep dip.

Derek There you go. Anyone of interest you never did want to interview them, did you?

Jo Maybe we're just interested in different things, Derek.

Derek Come on, then. Who's yours?

Jo Mine? Oh. Wait for it— (*Carefully*) Zyergefoovc——

Derek Never heard of it. What is it?

Jo A very famous surgeon. A professor——

Derek Male or female?

Jo Male.

Derek Young?

Jo Old.

Derek How old?

Jo Very, very, very old.

Derek Terrific.

Jo Not a great photo opportunity?

Derek Joking. (*With a sudden thought*) It's not his hundredth birthday, is it?

Jo Not quite.

Derek Pity. In my line, they've either got to be very, very nubile or very nearly dead.

Jo Well, I think we can now go our separate ways again, don't you? Goodbye. Off you go.

Derek I'm not going anywhere. I'm taking pictures here.

Jo Oh, no, you're not, I'm doing an interview out here.

Derek I won't get in your way.

Jo Derek, you can take pictures anywhere. There's acres of garden.

Derek So what? You can talk anywhere too, can't you?

They glare at each other

Jo God, you're still a bastard, aren't you? The day I kicked you out——

Derek laughs

—the day I kicked you out, that was the best decision I ever made.

Derek Kicked me out? I left, darling. I walked out.

Jo What are you saying? I threw your clothes in the street...

Derek Yes, and I stood there in the road and I kept saying "Jo, for the last time, are you coming with me? Yes or no"... Begging you to come with me.

Jo Begging me to be let in again...

Derek Not at all... Come on, that's not the way things were, Jo, you know it. You're just the same, you can't face something, you make it up...

Jo That is totally untrue, that is a lie...

Derek Come on, Jo, it's your creative imagination again, girl. It'll be the death of you one day, you know.

Jo *(loudly)* Derek, just go away and leave me alone!

The fierce nurse appears at the window of the empty room. She is holding a folded sheet

The nurse glares at them

(Penitently, to the nurse) Sorry.

Derek *(to the nurse)* Sorry, darling. She was just testing her microphone.

The nurse goes

A pause

God, Jo, you look a mess.

Jo Thanks.

Derek Hasn't anyone else remarked on it?

Jo Who is there to remark on it?

Derek I don't know. People at work?

Jo Why should they remark on it? They don't even notice me, most of them.

Derek They used to in my day.

Jo When?

Derek When we were together. On *The Advertiser*. People were always looking at you.

Jo Who were?

Derek Men.

Jo What men?

Derek All sorts of men. Men in the street. Men at work. I was dead jealous.

Jo I never noticed.

Derek The men?

Jo You being jealous.

Derek You used to look—you know, really good. What's happened?

Jo I'm older, Derek.

Derek Older? What are you? Thirty? That's not old. I'm only thirty-four. Thirty? That's the same age as Angie Dell. Look at her.

Jo Oh, well, if you're going to compare me to her...

Derek Look, how much do you weigh now, Jo? Tell me what's your weight these days...

Jo Mind your own bloody business...

Derek What are you, twelve stone? Thirteen, are you?

Jo I don't know. I never weigh myself.

Derek Fourteen.

Jo I'm not fourteen, certainly.

Derek Well, you'll have to do something about it before you keel over... What's the problem? Over-eating? Obviously.

Jo (*reluctant to talk about it*) Not really. I put on a bit of weight when I stopped smoking, that's all.

Derek Well, at least you've stopped smoking...

Jo I haven't really. I've started again.

Derek Terrific. You still drinking?

Jo Occasionally.

Derek Occasionally?

Jo Now and then.

Derek Now and then like every night?

Jo Some nights... What are you trying to do?

Derek Still on the beer?

Jo Yes.

Derek Halves?

Jo (*grimly*) Pints.

Derek Jesus. And a double pork pie to wash it down, I suppose?

Jo Oh, just shut up! It's my body, I'll do what I damn well like with it, OK?

Pause

Derek And you bite your nails, don't you?

Jo sticks her tongue out at him. She sits and rummages in her bag. She produces a bar of chocolate and defiantly starts to eat it. She is very unhappy

What's that?
Jo (*her cheeks bulging*) A Mars bar. Get stuffed.
Derek God help us.

Angie steps out on to the terrace from her room. She has now upped the image. A little added make-up and a chic summer dress

Angie Right, let's get it over with. Where do you want me?
Derek Oh, you should have kept your nightie on, Angie.
Angie I just told Ronnie about this and he's not happy, I tell you.
Derek Oh, dear. (*He steps down on to the lawn*) Could we try one on the steps?
Angie Yes, well, you just keep it level. You're not pointing it up my skirt, I can tell you that... (*She notices Jo*) Who's that?
Derek Oh—just a passing bag lady. Take no notice of her.

Jo, munching grimly through her Mars bar, glares at them both

(*Getting to work*) That's lovely, one there. That's beautiful, one just there. Great. Beautiful. Beautiful. Good girl.
Jo (*disgusted at Angie's antics*) God, honestly. Look at you both. It's obscene.
Angie Pardon?
Derek It's all right, she's run out of meths, that's all. Poor old thing. Walk, walk for me. That's it. Walk walk, sexy walk.

Angie minces up and down, hips gyrating

Jo (*muttering, sourly*) I don't know why they all have to walk in that stupid way, either. (*She fans herself*)

They ignore her. Derek continues to take his pictures. Angie goes through her well-rehearsed routine, posing and pouting

As they continue, Ronnie comes out on to the terrace via Angie's room, on his mobile phone

He covers the mouthpiece

Ronnie The next call I am making, will be to your editor, Mr Small. All right?

Derek (*without pausing*) Thank you very much, Mr Weston. That will be most helpful in confirming my expenses.

Benjamin comes on to the lawn, followed by Hravic and Freya

Benjamin Found them, found them at last... (*He sees the photo session in progress*) Now, what is going on here? I'm sorry, this clinic has a firm rule, absolutely no photographers under any——
Derek It's all right. Don't you mind us, squire. It's all official. (*To Ronnie*) Isn't it?

Ronnie shakes his head and goes inside to resume his phone call

Angie We won't be long, Benjamin.
Derek Just a couple more.
Benjamin (*unhappily*) Well, it really isn't...
Hravic (*eyeing Angie with ill-concealed lust*) Imst Skeet! Glarget brotten utternibbles! Butterscutt. [My God! Behold those bosoms. Unbelievable.]
Freya (*sourly*) Broodle! Broodle, har offle critzsnepper! [Behave! Behave, you old sex maniac!]
Benjamin Miss Knapton, may I introduce Professor Zyergefoovc. Hravic, this is Miss Knapton, from our local radio station.
Freya Britt gool Miss Knapton, ut scrittle bint u luke runtootshtickbeakle.
Jo (*hastily swallowing the last of her chocolate*) How do you do?
Hravic Een harnet meenus britt zim. [I could have done without this one.]
Jo (*shaking his hand*) How do you do, Professor.
Hravic Ip gool mankst vint ut bonzabatter. [She is made like a tank.]
Freya Gooch! [Quiet!]
Benjamin And this is Miss Roope, who will be translating for you. (*He smiles at Freya*)
Jo Hallo.
Freya Freya Roope.
Jo Jo Knapton.

They shake hands

Freya You are hot. Your hands.
Jo (*self-consciously*) Yes, sorry. Warm day.
Benjamin (*indicating the terrace*) Perhaps we should sit along here, out of the camera's way. (*He squeezes past Derek and Angie*) Excuse me...
Derek Carry on, squire. Don't mind us.

Derek and Angie continue their photo session unperturbed. Benjamin and party make their way to the terrace

Benjamin (*as they do this*) Hravic is happy to remain outside, is he?

Freya Gult har limlim gripper hrossich? [Are you happy to stay outside?]

Hravic Har gult mut timmie. [You must be joking.]

Benjamin (*arranging the seating*) Well, now, Hravic, would you like to sit here?

Freya Set har hoot? [Sit you here?]

Hravic (*indicating the other chair, facing Angie*) Noot, een fiss utternibbles looper. [No, I want to watch the bosoms.]

Freya He would rather sit here and not looking into the sun.

Benjamin Oh, yes, just as he prefers. Is this chair all right for you, Miss Knapton?

Jo That's fine. So long as I can reach them both with the mic.

Freya I will sit next to him here.

Hravic (*sniffing the air, distastefully*) Ip pookt vint ut pokenstabiel. [She smells like a whorehouse.]

Jo What's he saying?

Freya He says you have strong perfume.

Jo Oh, it's just cologne. Does he object?

Hravic (*wrinkling his nose*) Mousse inzerzooty. [Very unpleasant.]

Freya He doesn't mind at all.

Benjamin I'll sit just here, if you don't mind...

Jo (*dismayed*) Oh, really? You don't have to if you have things to——

Benjamin I'd prefer it, if you don't mind. Just in case there are language difficulties—and so on.

Jo Just as you wish. Well, shall we go straight in? (*She looks at the others*)

They are all three watching Angie and pay Jo little attention at all from this point on

(*Ironically, to herself*) Yes, I suppose we might as well. I'll just check things are working. (*She fiddles with the recorder*)

Derek continues to talk encouragingly to Angie, coaxing her into new poses

(*Speaking into the mic*) Jo Knapton interview with Professor Zyergefoovc, thirteenth of July... (*Angrily to Derek*) Could we keep the noise down a little, please. We are trying to record here.

Derek Sorry.

Jo Thank you. May I have a word or two for level? For level? Some words.

Freya You want some words?

Jo Yes, please.

Freya What words are these?

Benjamin She wants some words for testing, Freya.

Freya Oh, testing words. Hallo, hallo, hallo, hallo. That's all right?

Jo Thank you very much. Could…?

Freya Ip fenkt um zooper far winkie. [She wants some words for testing.]

Hravic Ah! Winkiezooper. Utternibbles. Airgroom dumble utternibbles. [Ah! Test words. Bosoms. Huge bouncing bosoms.] (*He laughs*)

Freya Not translatable.

Benjamin "Dumble" I think means leaping or bouncing. Bouncing. Yes, literally bouncing freely. But utternibbles—I haven't come across. It may be a medical word. Elbows, possibly.

Freya No, they are not elbows. Bouncing elbows, no.

Jo (*having checked her machine*) Yes, right. Shall we start? Ready? Good. (*She is getting slightly testy at the lack of attention*) If we could tear ourselves away from the cabaret. From the utternibbles.

Hravic (*smiling at her*) Utternibbles … yes…

Jo Yes, I thought that would get your attention… Professor Zyergefoovc, may I first of all welcome you to this country…

Freya (*translating swiftly as Jo speaks*) Yippy bit britt England…

Jo …and to say what a pleasure it is to have such a distinguished man of medicine visiting our shores…

Freya Wet zooter ip gool ribbics ut keetyzitt estemental bit vipper sucks…

Hravic (*bored*) Lololo. Gittle. Gittle. [All right. Get on with it. Get on with it.]

Freya (*translating back*) He says thank you, you're very kind.

Hravic Imst Skeet! Glarget brutt teadle! Ip gool ut cusherteadle. [My God! Look at that bottom. It's a classic bottom.]

Jo I'm sorry?

Freya Not translatable.

Hravic Een fiss gitter imst putts in brutt. (*He chuckles*) [I want to get my hands on that.]

Jo (*muttering*) Yes, he's a jolly old gentleman, isn't he? (*To Hravic*) Professor, if I could tear you away from nature for a minute, this is your first trip to the West in thirty years, isn't it?

No reply

Yes, it is. Why did you choose to come here to the Othman Clinic?

Freya Eep tuttilt har bit Othman Clinic loot groat?

Hravic Tott ip bit stooperdick. [Tell her to mind her own business.]

Freya He says there are many complicated reasons but mainly his great affection for Mr Benjamin Cooper, his once student and now friend who has supported Professor Zyergefoovc for so long during his sad separation from this country which he himself grew to love when he came to teach here all those many years ago. Professor Zyergefoovc still retains a great affection and respect for the British people and most especially for the British medical profession which in his opinion is second to no-one in the world.

Jo Yes.

Benjamin (*appreciatively as he watches Angie*) My word!

Jo (*irritably*) What?

Benjamin Sorry. Nothing.

Jo Since he returned to his own country, we are given to understand that Professor Zyergefoovc made enormous strides in surgical techniques. Techniques which far outstrip anything we've managed to achieve in this country.

Freya Yes, he has. I can answer that.

Jo Could you ask him, would he be prepared to discuss any of those breakthroughs?

Freya Gult har totter harg breakthroughs hroomper?

Hravic Breakthroughs hroomper? Noot. Nord bit ut zump keet onfild tokenstrappel. [Medical breakthroughs? No. Not to a fat idiot woman journalist.]

Freya Not possible, I'm afraid. The techniques are too difficult to discuss.

Benjamin (*still watching Angie*) Oh, my word.

Jo (*profoundly irritated*) Did you say something?

Benjamin No, no. I do beg your pardon.

Jo Derek, are you going to be much longer?

Angie No, he isn't.

Jo Because it's getting very difficult here.

Derek One more minute.

Hravic Quest ip, britt tonkenstrappel, eep nord dorpt clinter. [Ask her, this journalist, why she doesn't diet?]

Freya smiles at this

Jo What did he say?

Freya He asks why you don't bother to diet?

Jo I beg your pardon. Why I don't what?

Hravic Hratt ip ten copple sit gobble, ip shimpt negeether?

Freya He asks, do you hate your body so much that you ignore it?

Jo I'm sorry, I don't think that has anything to do with anything.

Freya Nord ip ondt. [She won't answer.]

Hravic Lololo! Nit im. Ip gool crack, men. Int klingt ip ribbt shickershack snoop ipper smoot? [No! Nor would I. It's sad, though. Does she know she has chocolate round her mouth?]

Freya He says he doesn't blame you. But all the same, it's sad. And did you know you had chocolate all around your mouth?

Jo mops her mouth with her hand

Hravic Ut onfild sic binzt ten copple...
Freya A woman should care for her body.
Hravic (*indicating Angie*) Vint ip...
Freya Like her...
Hravic U copple iff ut onfild gool ut ester...
Freya The body of a woman is an altar...
Jo Oh, Jesus...
Hravic Croat far ut dent clayhruit...
Freya Built for a man to worship at...
Jo I don't believe this. Do you believe this?
Freya Me? No, I don't believe it, I think he's a stupid old man, I'm just telling you what he's saying, that's all.
Jo Tell him he's twenty years out of date.
Freya He's a hundred years out of date, what are you talking about? He's never been in date. Who cares, he's eighty-four years old. Forget it. He thinks I'm a lesbian because I don't run up his trousers whenever he whistles.
Hravic (*indicating Freya*) Ip gool ut hrootpucker. (*He laughs*) [She's a dyke.]
Jo Well, if he doesn't mind putting up with a few more questions from this overweight interviewer...
Freya Don't worry. Don't let him worry you. Fat women are good. In my country, we say marry a fat woman. They are always jolly and warm in winter.
Jo Oh well, that's a great consolation, thank you. Professor, I realize you're reluctant to discuss your work—especially the technical aspects—but you must be aware, I'm sure, that some of your experiments have attracted considerable interest in this country. Particularly your more controversial ones...
Benjamin Ah, now, now...
Freya I don't think he wishes to talk about that...
Jo Not in detail, but I'm sure he has some feelings about it. In the pursuit of his work, distinguished as it is, he's performed experimental surgery not only on animals but also, so we're led to believe, on human beings...
Benjamin Ah, now, now, now. I think we're rather straying out of bounds here...
Jo He has no feelings on the matter, then? He doesn't care either way. Arms, legs, heads transplanted, that doesn't trouble him?
Hravic Wet quest ip? [What's she asking?]
Freya Ip quest op harg insterpairogruntal tog. Ip nord duckt. [She's asking about your experimental work. She doesn't like it.]

Hravic So? Ip gool insterpairogruntal. Hrenst ip ut dimple? [So? It's experimental. Does she think it's a game?] (*He suddenly and unexpectedly leans forward and speaks to Jo directly and in English*)

Jo is startled

(*With difficulty*) The—work—that—I—doing—is impottant work. It is above a game. It is not for politics. It is not for— (*He hesitates, looking at Freya*) Wet gool leekletter?

Freya Laymen.

Hravic Laymen. (*Stabbing at Jo with his finger*) It is not for little vat journalist to question.

Derek's attention is suddenly caught by this last sentence. He stops photographing Angie and turns to look at Hravic

Jo (*hostile*) You feel you're above the law then?

Hravic Wet?

Freya Effer u rundel?

Hravic Jit. Insterbeat.

Freya Yes, absolutely.

Jo Perhaps he feels he's God?

Freya Gult har Skeet?

Hravic Keet gool dent it dent gool keet, eek klingt?

Freya God is man or man is God, who knows?

Jo Yes, that's a pretty handy answer, isn't it? Covers most things.

Derek Now I know who he is. It's him.

Angie Who?

Derek starts to take pictures of Hravic furiously

Benjamin Yes, well, I think we've reached a convenient point to stop, don't you? I was going to suggest a glass of sherry perhaps...

Freya Ut tink iff sherry.

Hravic Ah, sherry! Dillditch! [Ah, sherry! Delicious!]

Jo Just a second, we haven't finished...

Benjamin I think Professor Zyergefoovc has said all he wants to say. You have already exceeded your brief. (*He rises*)

Jo He hasn't said anything.

Angie (*to Derek*) Finished with me, I take it?

Derek Thank you.

Angie Any time.

Freya Bim hrissich? [Coming inside?]

Hravic Jit, jit. Hrissich.

They continue, overlapping the others' dialogue

Ert zimter, een fiss shrigger Memmer Utternibbles woo ten benshtergeel teadle. Oh, een woot vint ipper ribbics. [But first, I want to speak to Miss Breasts with her beautiful bottom. Oh, I would like to have her.]

Freya Bonker offle keet. Har kist nord ip mageler. [Silly old idiot. You couldn't manage it.]

Hravic Zim bed, Memmer Hrootpucker, zim bed. Har zinct. [One day, Madame Dyke, one day. You'll see.]

Freya Hooray!

Angie (*rather put out*) Who is that old man, anyway?

Derek (*still taking pictures*) He's that surgeon, you know. The one who sews dogs' heads on pigs and all that. That one.

Angie Ugghhh!

Jo I've hardly recorded anything at all down here.

Benjamin I'm sorry, that's the best we can do for you. You had your chance, he's a very busy man...

Jo But surely——

Benjamin Why don't you talk to Miss Dell? I'm sure she'd love to be interviewed. Now, you must excuse us——

Jo Well, terrific. Thanks very much.

Derek (*still happily filming away*) Blown it again, eh, Jo?

Jo Oh, shut up.

Benjamin has stopped and is studying the sky

Benjamin Helicopter.
Hravic Wet?
Freya (*pointing*) Hottiefingertetter.
Hravic Oh, jit. Hottiefingertetter.
Angie Heliocopter.
Derek Yes. (*He starts to photograph it*)

We can now hear the sound of its engines which grow increasingly loud

Benjamin Good Lord, I think it's going to land here, on the lawn. It can't do that. (*He calls to the helicopter*) I say... I say...

His voice is drowned out by the din. They all stand and watch

One or two nurses appear in the rooms to watch as well. Ronnie also appears

He shouts to ask what's happening but no-one can hear him. The wind from the blades becomes apparent. Jo clutches her notes. The machine apparently lands. The sound of the rotors slowing down

Who on earth can it be?
Jo (*to Derek*) More of your friends, I presume?
Derek No, they'd never have landed.
Angie Oh God, it's him. It's Mal. It's bloody Mal.
Derek Hey, it is. It's Mal Bennet. Fantastic. (*He runs forward*) Hold it there, Mal, lovely. That's perfect.

Derek goes off momentarily

Angie How the hell did he find me? (*To Ronnie*) Did you tell him?
Ronnie Never.
Benjamin Mal—who is it?
Jo Mal Bennet. He's a pop musician.
Benjamin Oh.
Freya Mal Bennet—pop clanker.
Hravic (*unimpressed*) Ah jit, pop clanker. Lololo…

Mal appears. Leather jacket and designer jeans. He is a living triumph of image over age. A fifty year old who manages, usually, to look twenty-five. He carries a gift-wrapped box

A scream from the nurses

Mal (*acknowledging them*) How do you do?
Benjamin Now, will everyone please get back to work, immediately. (*To Mal*) And will you be so kind as to move that thing at once, please…
Mal (*totally ignoring him*) Ange!
Angie I'm not speaking to you, Mal.
Mal Ange!
Angie You've had it.
Mal Ange!
Benjamin Do you hear me? Will you kindly move that machine off the lawn?
Mal Angel!
Benjamin There is newly planted grass seed out there…
Mal (*holding up the box*) I brought you a present, Angel.
Angie I don't want your sodding present…
Derek Could you just hold the box up again, Mal?
Mal (*doing so*) Angie!

Derek That's it. Ta. Lovely, Mal.

Benjamin Now listen, I am in charge here and I will not be ignored. You will either move that helicopter at once or I will call the police.

Mal Who is this? Who is this git?

Angie Don't you shout at him. He's my medical adviser.

Mal Well, bugger off.

Benjamin (*approaching Mal angrily*) Now, listen, don't you take that tone with me, young man, I don't care who you are…

Angie Young man? That's a joke.

Derek Just hold it like that, gentlemen. That's lovely.

Angie He was touring with Bill Haley, he was…

Hravic Eek gool Bill Haley? [Who is Bill Haley?]

Freya Bill Haley gool ut offle pop clanker. [Bill Haley is an old pop singer.]

Hravic (*unimpressed*) Ah, jit. Ut offle pop clanker. [Ah, yes. An old pop singer.]

Mal Look, back off, all right. Just back off. No trouble, all right.

Benjamin I think you may have just found it, my friend…

Ronnie Now, listen, listen. Gents. Might I suggest? Two very valuable equally talented people, not worth the fisticuffs. Ben—Mr Ben, friend. Let Mal have five minutes with Angie, that's all he came for, isn't it, Mal…?

Mal That's all I came for. I didn't come here for spillage.

Angie I'm not having five minutes with him…

Ronnie Angie!

Angie I'm not having five seconds…

Ronnie Angie! It's that or the police. Now, none of us want that.

Angie Where's the law that says I have to sit down and listen to him…

Mal I'm not into spillage…

Ronnie Ladies and gents, shall the rest of us go inside? I think we should, don't you? You too, Derek. Leave the husband and wife alone.

Benjamin Five minutes. Then I want that thing off the lawn.

Ronnie Five minutes, that's all he wants.

Angie That's all he's getting…

Benjamin Hravic, my friend, come along… Sherry, everyone. Miss—er— Knapton, would you…?

Jo Yes. Thank you.

Ronnie Miss Knapton, are you Miss Knapton?

Jo Yes.

Ronnie There was a call for you. I took it on the public phone there. Can you call your office.

Jo Oh, right. I switched mine off. Thank you.

Jo follows Benjamin, Hravic and Freya indoors

Hravic (*as they go, pointing at Mal*) Brutt gool Bill Haley?

Freya Noot, noot, noot... Nord Bill Haley.

They go off

Ronnie takes the reluctant Derek by the arm

Ronnie Come on.
Derek Any chance of you kissing each other?
Mal Sure.
Angie No way.
Ronnie Come on.

Ronnie and Derek go in

Angie and Mal are alone. A silence

Angie Well?
Mal I need you. I want you. I've got to have you. I've tried it without you.
I've tried it with other people. I've tried it on my own. I've tried it with like,
you know, groups of people. I've tried it with friends. I've tried it with, you
know, strangers, you know. I've tried it with—you name it. And in the end,
Angie—it's got to be with you.
Angie No, it hasn't.
Mal So.
Angie No.

Pause

  No.

Pause

Mal No?
Angie Yes.

Pause

  Like no. Understand?

Pause

Mal Well.
Angie Where'd you get the 'copter?

Mal I—borrowed it.

Angie I didn't know you could fly one.

Mal No, well, this feller showed me.

Angie Who?

Mal Oh, you know—I can't remember his name. Used to play with the Four Apostles—oh, whatsisname...?

Angie Matthew?

Mal No.

Angie Mark?

Mal No. Keep going...

Angie Not Luke?

Mal Jim. That's the one.

Angie Oh, Jim. I didn't know Jim could fly.

Mal Oh, yes. Sometimes.

Pause. Neither of them move

I mean, we're still married, you see...

Angie Yes, I know. We'll need a divorce, won't we?

Mal No, I meant...

Angie We'd better get that organized.

Mal No. I still want you, you see.

Angie Well, Mal. That's too bad, isn't it?

Mal You don't want me?

Angie No. Not at all.

Mal Did you ever want me?

Angie Mal, you know what I feel like about all that side. I can take it or leave it, it doesn't make all that difference. I know with you, it's like the end of the world if you're not having it once a minute, but it really doesn't do much for me, you know it doesn't. I'm sorry. That's the way I'm made.

Mal Perhaps if we tried again? I might arouse you this time.

Angie Mal, you tried everything there is, love. Give it up. God love us, you nearly ruptured yourself trying. I'm just no... I could be frigid, I suppose, I don't know. Probably. I'm sorry. And I'm sorry I hit you with the lamp.

Mal No, that's...

Angie Look, go on, Mal. Go on home and have a few people, you'll feel better.

Mal *(crestfallen)* Nobody like you, Ange. There's none of them like you.

Angie Bye!

Mal Bye!

Mal starts to leave

Angie Oy! Don't I get my present?

Mal Oh, yes. Here. (*He gives her the parcel*)

Angie What is it?

Mal Have a look.

Angie (*opening the parcel*) Whatever is it? (*She gazes at the contents, delighted as a kid*) It's a book.

Mal Yes.

Angie (*touched*) Oh, Mal. Did you go and buy it?

Mal Yes.

Angie On your own?

Mal Yes.

Angie Oh, Mal.

Mal I remember you saying you wished someone would buy you a book for a change. Instead of—you know—jewellery and knickers and that...

Angie Yes, I remember. I did.

Mal I haven't read it, but I heard it was good.

Angie Great. Fantastic. Thank you. Thanks very much. (*She clutches the book to her, like a child with a new toy*)

Mal Live long, Ange, all right?

Angie Yes.

Mal goes down the steps. He takes one last look at her and then goes off towards his helicopter

(*Reading the cover*) Crime—and—Punishment by—(*Squinting*)—Dost—oh, God! Somebody or other. Where the hell did he find this?

Jo comes out on to the terrace through the empty room. She looks out cautiously and sees Angie is alone

Jo Er... Hallo.

Angie (*rather coolly*) Yes?

Jo (*taking a deep breath*) I'm sorry to trouble you—I wouldn't do this normally but my news editor has just phoned. He's asked if I can get an interview with you. I don't know how he found out you were here, I promise you it wasn't me and I'm very sorry. Would you spare me five minutes to talk? Only I think otherwise I could be getting the sack.

Angie Talk?

Jo Yes. About anything you like.

Angie For the radio?

Jo Yes.

Angie No pictures?

Jo None at all.

Angie Fine.

Jo You will?

Angie Why not?

Jo Thank you. Thank you so much. Well. Shall we...? (*She indicates that they sit*) What's that you're reading?

Angie Oh—(*She checks the title*) *Crime and Punishment*.

Jo (*surprised*) Oh, Dostoevsky.

Angie Dostoevsky. Yes.

Jo Wonderful book.

Angie Yes. I haven't started it yet.

Jo It's great.

Angie (*holding the book*) Yes, it is. Brilliant.

The sound of the helicopter being started. Angie suddenly bounds up

   Excuse me... (*She starts to go*)

Jo Where are you going?

Angie (*as she goes*) I just want to say goodbye to my husband...

Jo Well, don't get too...

The sound of the helicopter drowns her voice. Angie stands on the lawn and jumps up and down trying to attract Mal's attention

Angie Mal! Bye bye, Mal. Mal! Mal!

Mal evidently fails to hear her. Jo watches her apprehensively

   (*Waving her arms*) Mal! Mal!

The helicopter engine revs. More slipstream

   Angie runs forward towards it and out of view, shouting inaudibly as she goes

Jo (*rising in alarm*) Look out, don't go near to the—Miss Dell! Angie! Oh, my God!

Jo, with a surprising burst of agility, leaps off the terrace and sprints after Angie

One awful cry. It is Mal's voice. The engines gradually stop. Silence

Everyone arrives on the terrace at once. Through Angie's room come Ronnie and Derek. From the other room, Benjamin followed a little way

*behind by Freya and Hravic. They all arrive at the windows and stop short
at the sight of what they see*

Benjamin (*horrified*) Oh, no. No, no.
Ronnie (*very faint*) Aaah!
Freya Eeech!
Hravic Yet!
Derek Shit!

*Benjamin starts to move forward. Ronnie stands, a man in a daze. Derek
follows Benjamin, equally stunned. He barely seems to have the strength to
lift the camera to his eye. Somehow he manages it*

Freya Grooth! Grooth! [Bad! Bad!]
Ronnie Oh, dear God. Angie... (*He sways and looks very ill*)

Hravic and Freya watch the scene for a moment

Hravic (*suddenly, excitedly shouting*) Noot! Noot! Benjamin! Sneetilt u
  tooter! (*He moves towards the direction of the accident with unaccustomed
  alacrity*)

Freya starts to follow

Benjamin! Sneetilt u tooter!

Hravic goes off

Ronnie (*startled*) What's he saying?
Freya (*going*) He says, to save the heads...

Freya goes after Hravic

Ronnie (*incredulously*) Save the heads? Save the *heads*?

*Ronnie cannot contain himself a second longer. He rushes back into the
house to throw up*

As he does so, the Lights change to denote the passing of time

SCENE 2

It is another morning, some weeks later. Slightly more overcast perhaps, but still pleasantly mild

There is activity in both the rooms. nurses bustle to and fro with bowls and dressings, medical paraphernalia

Benjamin appears from what was originally Angie's room, holding a clipboard. He is talking earnestly to someone out of our sight

Benjamin (*listening intently, and glancing from time to time at the clipboard*) Yes, yes. (*He listens*) Yes, yes, yes. (*He listens*) I see. Yes. (*He listens*) Yes. Yes. Yes. Yes. No. Yes. (*He listens*) Yes, I see. Good. Thank you.

A nurse leaps forward and takes the clipboard from him. Benjamin moves out on to the terrace

(*Thoughtfully, to himself*) Yes… Incredible.

A second later and Hravic emerges from the other room. He is also talking to someone we cannot see

Hravic Jit … jit … jit… Hroos.
Benjamin (*seeing him and extending both his hands*) Ah!
Hravic My friend!
Benjamin Hravic, my dear friend!
Hravic Benjamin, my dear friend.

They embrace

Benjamin Today out of danger, yes? Both?
Hravic Both?
Benjamin The two? No danger?
Hravic (*understanding*) No. No danger. One still—wet?— dringling… [weak]
Benjamin Dringling?
Hravic Jit… Dringling—Speck. [Limp] Wet? (*He calls impatiently*) Freya! Freya!

Freya comes from the room Hravic came from. She is wearing a doctor's coat

Freya Wet?

Hravic Wet tintics dringle on Anglish? [What does dringle mean in English?]

Freya Dringle tintics—er—Not strong. Weak.

Benjamin Ah, weak. One of them is still weak, yes.

Hravic Jit. Zim ribbt u flupt copple. Mroos hros iff minterglazer. [One has a very flabby body. Very out of condition.]

Freya Yes, one of them was very out of condition. Her body was very droopy—Yes?

Benjamin Droopy. Or flabby, yes. Both good words.

Hravic U atter, ipper copple gool vint u—tinzle.

Freya The other, her body is like a—good motor—a good machine. Beautiful!

Hravic Benshtergeel!

Freya Beautiful.

Hravic Pea far zim hos gool indivard ut drint iff umpergell...

Freya So for one there is always a risk of rejection...

Hravic U atter—hoos gool mins dool.

Freya For the other there is less worry.

Benjamin Good, good... Yes, I agree...

Hravic Stappleford ... stappleford ... far um breet, wits onfilder ribber ut airgroom vissertooth bruger. [Fortunately ... fortunately ... for some reason, both women have a huge desire to live.]

Freya Fortunately, for some reason both of them seem to have a very strong will to live.

Benjamin Yes, yes, yes... Nevertheless, Hravic, you have performed a miracle.

Freya Ip ditts, dar ribbilt makst ut patterstill...

Hravic (*modestly*) Patterstill? Noot, noot patterstill...

Benjamin I never believed it possible, dear friend...

Freya (*to Hravic*) Nord ip cradlt, gillt wasser.

Hravic Noot wasser? (*Wagging a finger*) Ah, Benjamin! Oh, har iff tinny dwindle...

Freya He says, oh, you of small faith...

Hravic laughs and embraces Benjamin, kissing him on both cheeks

Benjamin (*greatly embarrassed by this*) Yes, yes. Thank you.

Hravic stands back and smiles at Benjamin contentedly

Hravic Bat gool hroos, eh, Benjamin? Urt imst ettle, maddler ribbics pea gobble finn ploos u copplers onfilders stoot. (*He laughs*)

Freya Oh, gooch. Gooch.

Benjamin What does he say?

Freya Oh, his jokes. Always. Terrible jokes. He says how lucky he is that at his age he can still have such fun with women's bodies. That's funny, I don't think so. (*To Hravic*) Nord finnic.

Hravic (*playfully*) Ah! Har gult bangle, Memmer Hrootpucker. [Oh, you're jealous, Madame Dyke.]

Freya (*muttering*) Oh, zim bed! Zim bed! [Oh, one day! One day!]

Benjamin, feeling a bit left out of all this, laughs heartily. Hravic moves away from them, taking the air

Benjamin Freya—perhaps you could sound out Hravic, when you have a moment, as to when precisely he feels the press can be let in on this?

Freya The press?

Benjamin Yes. It's getting rather urgent. Obviously it's been possible for us over the past few weeks to fob them off with simple statements, but, now, with the strong possibility of at least one—if not both of them— regaining consciousness within the next day or so… We're going to have to let the press have something more substantial. If they suspect we're keeping anything back, they'll probably break the doors down—extra security guards or not.

Freya I will talk to Hravic. I know he would like both operations successful before he makes announcements.

Benjamin Wouldn't we all? But every day we procrastinate… (*He gesticulates*)

Freya Ask him now… Why not?

Benjamin Splendid. (*Tenderly*) You've been so helpful through all this, Freya. You really have. Thank you.

Freya No problem. (*She calls*) Hravic!

Hravic has reached the lawn

Hravic Wet? Wet?

Freya Vip fenkie har questic. [We want to question you.]

Hravic Eep. Een ticks grerb. Lesser. [Why? I am walking now. Later.]

Freya Noot, nord lesser. Grerb. Vip fenkie har questic grerb. [No, not later. We want to question you now.]

Hravic Lololo! Lololo! [All right! All right!]

He continues to move away, though, leaving them to catch him up as he totters off along the lawn

Benjamin It's just a very quick question, Hravic, I promise you, old friend…

Benjamin and Freya follow Hravic off

A pause

> *From Angie's room a figure uncertainly lurches into view. It is Jo. She is in a long, full length hospital gown which flaps loosely about her. It's impossible to see the shape of her body in detail. Her neck is heavily bandaged making it hard for her to move her head, certainly impossible for her to look down. Her hair has apparently been cut off. Her head is covered with a tight-fitting cap. She is dazed and bewildered*

She steps out on to the terrace and stops as she feels the cold stone under her feet. She makes a throaty gurgling sound. All presumably she can manage

Jo Urrh. Gurg. Gurg. Urg! (*She touches her neck. The effort of trying to speak has evidently caused her some pain. Something about the feel of her body causes her to freeze. She explores her upper chest tentatively. Worriedly*) Urr. (*She starts to explore lower down her body, very tentatively. When she reaches her bosom, her expression becomes one of incredulity and then horror. She slowly holds both hands up to her face to look at them closely*) Weerrg! (*She starts to panic. She runs her hands, so far as she can, lower down her body exploring through the gown, her waist, stomach, bottom and thighs. It is now quite apparent that the new Jo goes in where the old Jo stuck out*)

> *As she's doing this, a second figure lurches out of the other room and on to the terrace. It is Angie—or at least some of Angie. She is dressed identically to Jo*

She, too, stops in the doorway as her feet touch stone

Angie (*reacting to the cold under her feet*) Urrg!
Jo (*seeing her*) Urrg!
Angie (*seeing Jo*) Urrg!
Jo (*trying to tell her something*) Urrg!
Angie Urrg?
Jo (*urgently*) Urrg. (*She points at Angie with both hands*)
Angie (*still bewildered and dazed*) Urrg?

Jo lifts her gown an inch or so and indicates for Angie to do likewise

Jo (*demonstrating*) Urrg! Urrg!
Angie (*getting the gist of what Jo is saying*) Urrg! Urrg! (*She takes hold of*

her own robe. Her arms brush what is for her a rather wider body than she is used to. Like Jo, she freezes and then starts to explore her body under her gown. We are able to make out the ample frame that was once Jo's. Angie's exploration becomes as frenzied as Jo's was a minute ago) Urrg! Urrg!

As the truth dawns on Angie, she looks at Jo pleadingly, a sort of "Please tell me I'm dreaming" expression on her face. Jo shakes her head with difficulty to confirm Angie isn't dreaming. The women stare at each other in horror. Angie takes hold of her robe and lifts it fractionally off the ground so that Jo may look at her. Jo does the same for Angie. As both women slowly lift their robes each in turn, an inch or so at a time, the Lights fade to Black-out leaving only their faces spot lit. The two women's voices are heard raised in a simultaneous, gurgling scream as their worst fears are confirmed

Angie ⎫ *(together)* Uuurrrrrg!
Jo ⎭

CURTAIN

ACT II

SCENE 1

The same, two days later. Morning again. The good weather continues. The birds sing

Simultaneously, two nurses wheel two wheelchairs out of the separate rooms. The occupants are, of course, respectively Jo and Angie. Both still have their necks bandaged, and wear woollen hats to protect their heads. Their bodies they keep well hidden, each for her own very different reason, under the blankets in which they are wrapped. They are both, we discover later, in their dressing gowns

The nurses park the wheelchairs, give their patients' blankets an unnecessary twitch and then bustle back inside the house again

The women sit miserably in their respective chairs. They meet each other's eye, exchange a mutual glare of loathing and look studiously away again. A pause. Neither looks at the other but stares fixedly into the distance across the lawn

After a moment, Benjamin comes out of one of the rooms

Benjamin (*brightly*) Ah, good. Good, good, good. Sorry if I'm interrupting. I thought it was high time we got you both together. So we can thrash this out. We can't spend the rest of our lives sulking in our rooms, can we? That won't get us far, will it?

A pause. Neither woman acknowledges his presence

No. I think Hravic—Professor Zyergefoovc will be along with Freya in just a moment. I sent someone to find them, anyway. They should be here. Any minute.

Another pause. He is very nervous

I would like to say this to both of you, now we are together. I know I've said it to you individually but—it can't be said often enough. This is—all—very unfortunate. I can't really stress how unfortunate it is. For us all. But, alas, even with such a precise and—scrupulously careful—highly disciplined skill such as—surgical practice, mistakes—tiny errors of judgement—small miscalculations—do occasionally—very, very rarely—now and then—happen. I'm not here to defend Professor Zyergefoovc. Indeed not. He needs no defence. His actions were never at any time improper—or indeed anything other than highly admirable and—er—unimaginably skilful. What he has achieved in replacing simultaneously not one but two previously severed heads, heads which had become entirely separated from their bodies, well, such an achievement can only be described in any language as remarkable. If proof were needed that Hravic Zyergefoovc is our greatest living surgeon, then proof there is here in duplicate. Speaking personally, it was both an honour and a privilege to have assisted him in the operation—operations. I stand humbled and in total awe of his skill. Through the beauty of his hands I feel that I have momentarily at least glimpsed divinity itself. (*He pauses, rather moved by his own speech*)

Neither of the women appear to share his emotion. Their faces remain set

I think weighing everything up, ladies, you should both be extremely grateful simply to be alive.

He pauses, unnerved by their continuing silence

(*Plunging on*) On the brighter side, we're managing to keep the sensation seekers at bay. Of course, everyone knows about the accident and, of course, the subsequent operations—we could never have kept those a secret, not with a member of the press actually on the premises at the time. But since then we've managed to keep people away to enable you both to recuperate and as a result no-one outside has, as yet anyway, been informed about the—mix up. That is still our little secret. Though how long it can remain so… Obviously your nearest and dearest have been told… We couldn't hope to deceive them—nor would we want to. Miss Dell, your manager Mr Weston and, of course, your husband Mr Bennet— (*He frowns slightly*) I hope that was wise. In your case, Miss Knapton, we weren't absolutely able to trace any nearest and dearest—I don't know if we've…? No? The point is, ladies, we have decisions to make that need to be made reasonably quickly. Perhaps I might outline the choices, as I see them?

No reply

Very well. Choice number one. And, if I may say so, medically and politically by far the most prudent—is to leave things as they stand—to indulge, if you like, in a little harmless deception as to the nature of the—unfortunate mix up. After all, it has been known for people to undergo quite drastic weight changes following major operations of this sort and I'm certain we could, between us all, concoct a thoroughly convincing story. I do urge you both, ladies, if only for the sake of the enormous debt of gratitude you must surely feel you owe both to Hravic Zyergefoovc and—in a smaller way—to the staff of this clinic, to agree to this course of action.

They don't reply

Well, those are the various choices as I see them. I'll leave you both to think about it. I'll see what's happened to Hravic. Then I suggest we all sit and discuss it sensibly. Don't you agree? Good. Now keep warm. Don't rush about. And try not to talk too much... I'll be back in a moment, ladies. (*He looks at them anxiously*) Yes.

Benjamin goes off along the lawn

The two women continue to sit, unmoving

Jo (*at last, speaking with difficulty*) If he thinks I'm going to spend the—rest of my life with this body—he's—joking.

Angie (*croaking indignantly*) What about me? Have you seen this thing?

Jo Of course I've seen it. It's mine.

Angie It's enormous. It's huge. It's everywhere you turn. It follows you about. It's revolting.

Jo Well, I miss it. I feel like a pipe cleaner.

Angie It sweats. Do you realize that? It actually sweats. It's sweating now.

Jo Of course it sweats. It's human. Human beings sweat, dear. Didn't you know? I realize yours doesn't but then maybe that's because it consists mainly of silicone.

Angie Bloody liar! That is muscle tone.

Jo I came across your little scars, dear. Sorry.

Angie Well, you had no business looking, that is my...

Jo Not any more it isn't.

Angie (*miserably*) It's mine. I don't want this one. It's all... By the way, there's a lump on your leg here, did you know? Should I get it looked at?

Jo Oh, no. That's my sebaceous cyst, it's quite harmless.

Angie (*feeling her leg, suspiciously*) Is it? You sure?

Jo Yes. Feel free to squeeze it, if you want to. Be my guest.

Angie looks nauseated at the thought

Well, it helps pass the occasional winter evening.

Angie (*revolted*) Uuurk! What are we going to do? We can't stay like this.

Jo No way. We are going to get him—to put us back as we were.

Angie Won't that be dangerous?

Jo I'd sooner be dead than stay like this, wouldn't you?

Angie starts to cry a little

Oh, don't start that, it's not going to help.

Angie (*still crying*) I'm so hungry. It gets so hungry. I've never eaten so much in my life.

Jo (*wistfully*) I used to love food. I can't eat anything now. Did you never eat at all?

Angie Yes, masses. Fruit and—muesli and——

Jo Raw carrot. I discovered that one. It's mad about that. It's not that I'm hungry. I just miss the taste.

Angie What if he won't operate again? If he says he won't?

Pause. Jo doesn't answer

What do we do then? Kill ourselves?

Jo I don't know. I honestly don't know. (*She nibbles her nails anxiously*)

Angie What are you doing?

Jo Thinking.

Angie Well, don't do that, do you mind?

Jo What?

Angie Bite my nails. It took me years to grow those nails, now cut it out...

Jo Oh, go to hell... They're my nails now.

Angie They are not. They are my nails. If you want to bite nails come over here and bite these. Look at them, they're horrible. God, it's all horrible, it's foul, it's a greedy, disgusting, sweaty, cyst-ridden thing. (*Hitting her body furiously*) I hate it, I hate it. Great wobbly fat lump of lard.

Jo (*rising, menacingly*) Don't you dare do that to my body, how dare you treat it like that?

Angie Get stuffed, I'll do what I like with it...

Jo Oh, no, you won't. You touch it again and I'll——

Angie (*rising to meet her*) You'll what? You'll do what? Come on. Have a try. You'll be sorry if you do. I've tackled them bigger than you, darling, I'm warning you.

Jo I wouldn't get too energetic. You're terribly out of condition, you know...

Angie I'm not, you know, I'm——

Jo Oh, yes, you are, you know...

Angie (*realizing, in sudden anger*) You bloody——

She makes a lunge for Jo who with her new, lightweight body evades her easily. Angie, unused still to her new bulk, spins, loses her balance and sits heavily. She sits panting

Jo Take it easy. Mind your stitches.
Angie My God, I'm knackered. What sort of body is this? Nothing works at all. It can't even stand up. (*She gets up and tries another lunge*)

Jo gets round behind her and restrains her

(*Struggling ineffectually*) Give me back my body ... give it me back. Do you hear?

Jo gently pulls her to a chair and seats her

Jo Mind your stitches. Watch your stitches. (*Soothing*) Now, Angie, quietly, now. Calmly.

Angie now exhausted, calms down

That's better. You're very strong, aren't I? I mean, I'm very strong, aren't you... Amazing. (*She looks at her body with some respect*)
Angie (*miserably*) I was. I was in fantastic condition.
Jo (*gently*) You still are, Angie. It's in terrific shape, don't worry.
Angie I loved that body. I really loved it. I took such care of it...
Jo (*rather ashamed*) Yes. I'm sorry. I rather hated mine of late, I'm afraid.
Angie That's bloody obvious. It feels like it's been unoccupied for years.

They are both deeply depressed

Jo (*pulling herself together*) Angie, listen. We'd better agree on a few things. The first is that we don't fight each other. Because if you try and hit me, you're only hitting you. And vice versa. You see? We're going to have to be friends. Or at the very least, not enemies. We're literally part of each other now. Angie, I promise that so long as I have it, I will look after and respect your body. All right? Will you promise to do the same with mine?

Angie sits miserably

Angie. We need to agree on this, don't you see? Don't you want me to look after this for you? Not bite its nails or fill it full of Mars bars or smoke it to death? Don't you want me to exercise it for you—or whatever it is you do with it? Take it for walks? God help me, I bet you take endless exercise, don't you? Yes, I can feel it already, itching to do press-ups. Don't you want me to do that for you?

Angie remains silent

God, Angie, you're getting much the better deal, you know. All I ask of you is you feed mine properly. Breakfast, lunch, supper... Plenty of snacks between meals, please. Reasonable amounts of booze, if you feel like it. It can take quite a bit with safety and still fend off the wallies. Bladder's hopeless though, you'll be going all night if you do drink too much. Smoke as much as you like, feel free—well, cut down on that if you're able to, but I'm not insisting. Angie, we need each other. We do. (*Softly*) Please.

Angie (*in a small voice*) All right.

Jo You agree?

Angie How long do we have to keep it up?

Jo Until we get switched back. If he did it once, he can do it again. Or till we die in the attempt.

Angie But what if he won't agree? What then?

Jo There is no way he can refuse us. He can't. Every woman has a basic right to her own body.

Angie (*after a moment's thought*) No. It's too dangerous. It's too risky.

Jo You don't mind staying like that? For the rest of your life.

Angie I can slim.

Jo Ha! With that body? Try it.

Angie At least I'm still alive.

Ronnie appears in Angie's room. He has a vast bunch of flowers

Ronnie (*speaking to someone we cannot see*) ...No, she doesn't appear to be here. (*He calls*) Ange! Angie!

Angie Oh, God. It's Ronnie. (*She makes a dive for her chair and covers herself with her blanket*) What's he going to say when he sees me?

Jo Want me to leave you?

Angie He can't see me like this. What's he going to say?

Ronnie steps out on to the terrace

Ronnie Ah! They're here, they're here. Our heroines, our women of the hour. Angie, Jo! You both look sensational. Angie, I love you. I want to eat you up, girl.

He bends and kisses Angie who remains hidden under the rug. As he does this, Ronnie deposits the flowers on Angie's lap, further hiding her from view

(*As he does this*) Angie! Angie, Angie, Angie!

Angie (*limply*) Hallo, Ronnie.

Ronnie Oh, you smell good, girl.

Angie I smell horrible.

Ronnie turns to Jo. He extends his arms to her

Ronnie Jo...

Jo Hallo.

Ronnie (*hugging Jo*) Jo, Jo. This is a beautiful moment, Jo.

Jo Yes.

Ronnie (*drawing back*) And may I say—this on you, looks sensational. I mean it, sensational.

Jo Thank you.

Ronnie If you don't mind my saying—a thousand per cent improvement, Jo. Am I right, Angie? What does one say? Sensational, eh?

Angie gives a convulsive sob. Ronnie, in his euphoric state, doesn't notice

Jo (*embarrassed by all this*) Well, I'll just pop into my room for a minute. If you'll excuse me.

Ronnie Of course, thank you, Jo. You're right. I do need to talk to Angie.

Jo See you later, Angie.

Angie (*utterly miserably*) Yes.

Jo moves to her room, her hips swaying

Ronnie (*delighted*) Angie! Angie! Look at the walk. Get a load of the walk. Sensational.

Jo (*pressing her hips, with a dignified revulsion*) I can assure you how this body chooses to behave has nothing whatsoever to do with me.

Ronnie (*playfully*) Looks like you've got things under control to me, Jo.

Jo (*looking at him suspiciously*) Oh, yes?

Jo goes inside, still trying to control her hips

Ronnie turns to Angie

Ronnie Ange, you're down. I sense you're down, girl. Why are you down? Alleluya, you're alive. Stand up and thank God on your bended knees. I know what it is, post—post what do they call it? Post natal. That's what it is.

Angie Natal? I haven't had a baby.

Ronnie Well, whatever.

Angie Mind you, I feel like I'm expecting triplets.

Ronnie They've kept this very quiet, Ange. There's been not a whisper in the press. About the mix up. Nothing. Beautiful job of security. A very sharp firm, this security firm. We've every reason to be grateful. I bought them all pen and pencil sets. To thank them. Very impressive just getting in here. Now, Angie, before we get to business—we must discuss one thing. Mal.

Angie Mal? What's he done now?

Ronnie First, the good news. He's better, he's considerably better...

Angie Better?

Ronnie But the bad news, I'm afraid, is he's still a long way from being totally better...

Angie Better from what?

Ronnie From what he was.

Angie What was he?

Ronnie From being dead.

Angie Dead?

Ronnie You didn't know?

Angie No.

Ronnie On stage. Middle of the concert. Swansea football ground. High on the gantry, one minute he's playing—next minute he's jumped. Thirty feet. Straight into one of the drum kits.

Angie What happened?

Ronnie Fortunately, he forgot to unplug his bass guitar before he jumped. Hanging there fifteen feet up from his lead. Bouncing up and down like a yo-yo. They had to switch off and cut him down.

Angie My God.

Ronnie Been under sedation ever since. He blames himself, you see, Angie. He blames himself for your accident.

Angie He bloody well should, it was his fault.

Ronnie Ange, Ange. The boy is in collapse. He needs to see you, Ange. See you're alive, know that you've forgiven him.

Angie I haven't forgiven him.

Ronnie Ange...

Angie I'll never forgive him for what he's done to me.

Ronnie But you'll see him, won't you?

Angie I presume that means he's already coming?

Ronnie Just as soon as he can walk. He's still having a little trouble with his balance. Now. To brighter things. On the career side. A lot of the jobs we had slated before your accident, I've managed to put into cold storage. Angie, you'd be amazed the number of people who said, if it's a case of six months waiting for Angie Dell or some inferior girl now this minute, we'll wait for Angie. Only the urgent ones I've had to let go——

Angie Ronnie, are you serious? You're not expecting me to carry on working?

Ronnie How do you mean?

Angie Ronnie, you must be joking. After what's happened to me. Who's going to want me now?

Ronnie Everybody wants you, I'm just saying…

Angie Not once they've seen me, they won't…

Ronnie What's wrong with you? I've seen you. You look a million dollars. What's different about you?

Angie Everything's different, you twit. Starting round about this point. (*She indicates the bandage round her neck*) I've got rivets through my skin. I look like the Bride of Frankenstein under here.

Ronnie I've thought of that. A simple black ribbon around the throat. Till it heals. Very simple, deeply sexy.

Angie Brilliant. And what about the rest of me, then?

Ronnie How do you mean?

Angie I mean this… Look at it. I mean, just take a good look at it, Ronnie. Feast your eyes. (*She stands up, pulling the blanket aside for him to see. Simultaneously she removes her cap to reveal her cropped head*)

Ronnie studies her critically for a moment

Ronnie (*at length*) The hair we can deal with. The hair's no problem.

Angie What hair are you referring to?

Ronnie On your head. Where else?

Angie You'd be surprised. This woman's got hair in all sorts of places.

Ronnie They make marvellous wigs these days. Walk up and down.

Angie I'm not walking up and down.

Ronnie (*sternly*) Angie, walk up and down.

Angie lumbers up and down, doing her best

Is that natural? Are you walking naturally?

Angie I'm doing my best. I'm not used to it, am I?

Ronnie You're walking like a sailor.

Angie I feel like a shipwreck.

Ronnie All right. Now, sit down.

Angie does so

Cross your legs.

Angie (*through gritted teeth*) I can't cross my legs. The first time I tried I nearly put my back out.

Ronnie All right. Let's have a look at the legs then.

Angie No way.

Ronnie Angie...

Angie No. No. That's it. Sorry, no legs. No tits and very definitely no bum. That is final, Ronnie. I mean it, OK?

Ronnie OK. Fair enough.

A pause. Ronnie ruminates. Angie watches him anxiously

Angie Well?

Ronnie Well. You're going to have to lose weight.

Angie Oh, God. Brilliant.

Ronnie In the meantime, I think I can get you outsize work. Big girls with pretty faces. They can do extremely well in mail order.

Angie Mail order?

Ronnie Fashions for the fuller figure. Foundation garments. That sort of thing.

Angie (*appalled*) Foundation garments?

Ronnie Just till you've slimmed down...

Angie I'd be the laughing stock of everywhere...

Ronnie Angie, it's work...

Angie I was a Page Three girl once...

Ronnie (*gently*) Not any more, Angie. Not any more.

A pause

I'm sorry, you must understand. In your present state not even you'd want to look at it. Why should anybody else? Big roly-poly girls. That's not what the public want. Me, I love big roly-poly girls. You've met my wife, Rita, she's huge.

Angie (*sulkily*) Well, I'm not doing corsets. That's out.

Ronnie Fuller figure fashions. Just till you're slim again. Once you're slim again, business as usual. I promise.

Angie (*bitterly*) Perhaps you should go and ask her in there. She might model for you.

Ronnie Who?

Angie Jo. If it's just my little body you want, why don't you see if she'll lend it you?

Ronnie Angie. There's one other serious ingredient, remember? Personality. And that, only you've got. There's a million girls with beautiful bodies and dead behind the eyes. Who needs them?

Angie About as many as need fat girls with sparkling personalities.

Ronnie (*moving off*) I'll be there with you, Ange. Every step of the way. Don't worry.

Angie Where you going?

Ronnie Just need to phone. I'll be back. Take the weight off your feet. Your
ankles'll swell. Like Rita's.

Ronnie exits

Angie Oh, great... (*She stands very depressed*) They can hardly swell up any
more, can they? God, I'm hungry. I'd kill for sausage, egg and chips.

Jo appears

Jo Has he gone?

Angie Phoning.

Jo Oh.

Pause

Angie Jo...

Jo Mmmm?

Angie I can't live like this. I'm sorry. I mean, the way people keep... The
thought of walking around with... After... Well, you get used to... You
know. I mean, I don't want to sound hurtful but...

Jo You want back?

Angie Or out? I'll risk it.

Jo Me too. (*She extends her hand*) Done?

Angie Done.

*They shake hands. Neither can resist an involuntary shudder as they touch.
The Lights change again to denote the passing of time*

Scene 2

The same. A few days later. Morning

*Angie comes out of her room. She is dressed—and though she still has her
bandage round her neck, it is slimmer, less cumbersome as if the dressing has
been reduced as the wound heals. Her choice of clothes is questionable.
Although evidently specially purchased for her, she has chosen, unsuccessfully,
to try and maintain her original image despite her different shape. A big
woman in a small woman's clothes. She holds a stopwatch in one hand and
carries a bag in the other*

She sets herself down in a chair with a grunt. She finds the weather uncomfortably hot. She pulls her clothes away from her body and fans herself with her hand. She burps gently. She consults the stopwatch

After a second, Jo comes running on along the lawn. Like Angie's, the bandage around Jo's neck is now slimmer. She wears a fetching tracksuit. It evidently belongs to Angie. We know this because it has Angie emblazoned on it, front and back

Jo (*breathless*) That it?

Angie It? You're joking. Another fifteen minutes, girl. Get going. Round twice more at least.

Jo Twice? (*She stands with her hands on her hips*)

Angie Don't stop. Keep running. Hup—hup—hup. It's not tired. I'll know when it gets tired.

Jo You do this every morning?

Angie Every morning. Except Sundays. Then I do it twice.

Jo Oh, God.

Angie Don't stop. Look at you. You're not even sweating. Off you go.

Jo This is murder. I'll die, I know I will, I'll just die.

Jo runs off

Angie Die. She's not even broken sweat, look at her. I'm the one that's sweating. I'm coated from top to bottom in anti-perspirant, an' all. I'm totally body-sealed. Beats me where it's all leaking out from. God, roll on winter. (*She holds her arms out from her body slightly to allow air to circulate*)

At that moment Freya comes out of Angie's room

Freya What are you doing? You are learning to fly?

Angie No. I'm just very hot.

Freya Of course. You are too fat.

Angie I know.

Freya Much, much too fat. You have a great strain on your heart. You should thin. Before you die.

Angie Yes, thank you.

Freya You eat like you want to die. I have watched you, in the staff canteen. Every morning, two breakfasts. Why is this? Four eggs is too much.

Angie I know. You tell her. Tell Jo, not me.

Freya Tell her what?

Angie Tell her not to eat so much.

Freya But she's not eating. It's you that are eating.

Angie I know but I'm eating for her.

Freya For her?

Angie Yes.

Freya Why is she not eating for her?

Angie Because she's eating for me.

Freya She's eating for you.

Angie Yes, we're eating for each other, you see.

Freya I see. (*She ponders*) No, I don't understand. I think this is not translatable.

Angie It's complicated.

Freya Uh-huh. A very warm day.

They stare out at the lawn

Jo jogs on momentarily and looks at Angie hopefully

Angie Keep going. Hours yet.

Jo gives a little moan and runs off

Freya You are the one who should be running. Not her.

Angie She's running for me.

Freya (*looking at her suspiciously*) Yes?

Angie (*deciding to change the subject*) How's the professor this morning? It must be wonderful to work for such a marvellous man, I should imagine.

Freya What are you talking about, it's hell on earth. There is nothing wonderful to say for him.

Angie Oh. Clever, though. You have to admire him.

Freya Oh, yes, you have to admire him, he insists that you do. But you don't have to like him. Nobody likes him. He is also cruel to me. You have no idea.

Angie (*sympathetically*) Is he? Is he?

Freya All the time. Little jibbs. Little cruel creases.

Angie Cracks.

Freya Cracks. He calls me all the time a hrootpucker. Me—a hrootpucker.

Angie (*disapprovingly*) Well...

Slight pause

What exactly is a hootpacker, then?

Freya A hrootpucker is a slang word. A very rude, insulting word. In our country no longer used. Forbidden. It means a—lesbian woman, you know?

Angie Oh, a dyke. We call them dykes here.

Freya Dykes. That is also insulting.

Angie Yes. I suppose it is.

Freya Hrootpucker. Dykes. What's the difference? It is diminishing to women.

Angie Yes.

A pause

You're not a hootpacker, are you?

Freya (*fiercely*) No, I am not a hrootpucker. Nor am I a dyke. Nor any of these things. Nor am I a bimbo which he has also recently learned to call me. (*Shouting*) I am a perfectly normal woman with normal functions, do you hear?

Angie (*alarmed by this outburst*) Yes, yes. I'm sorry.

Freya (*muttering*) In your language there are more words insulting women than in any other language. Did you know that?

Angie Really. Yes, I wouldn't be surprised. I think my father called me by most of them. Would you like a bit of Mars bar? (*She produces one from her bag*)

Freya No, no. Not Mars bars. No, no, no.

Angie (*setting it aside*) No, well, I have to eat them, you see.

Freya Hravic, he hates women. He really hates women.

Angie Well, I suppose I've still got to be grateful to him. He's a great surgeon, isn't he? Even if he is a dirty old man.

Freya He was a great surgeon. No more. You were lucky, believe me. In the last years he has had many failures.

Angie Has he?

Freya Oh, yes. Why do you think they let him come to the West? I tell you, there would soon have been no people left. Let him go, they said, let him murder the capitalists, not us.

Angie He's done human head transplants before, then, has he?

Freya Oh, yes. Many times. But not many times successfully.

Angie (*nervously*) Who were they all, then? Were they—were they all people like us who lost their heads in accidents, were they?

Freya How many people do you know who lose their heads in accidents?

Angie (*digesting this*) Oh...

Freya (*bitterly to herself*) Hrootpucker! One day. One day. He will learn the power of women's anger, this Hravic Zyergefoovc. Who thinks he's God. God who wants to look in women's skirts and expects them to worship him. Someone one day will do him to death. Maybe me, who knows?

Angie Wait till he's operated on us first, won't you?

Freya Operated? You want him to operate on you again? You're both crazy people.

Angie We're demanding that he does. He has to say yes.

Freya (*agitated*) You must not let him operate. I beg you. You must not make him.
Angie Every woman has the right to her own body.
Freya (*shouting*) You are mad. Do you know how close you came? How close?

Ronnie has come through Angie's room. He sticks his head through the door on to the terrace

Ronnie Er... Angie. (*He sees Freya*) Oh, do excuse me.
Freya (*rising, moving to leave*) Tell her. You tell her no. No, no, no, no, no. This mad monkey.

Freya goes

Ronnie looks rather startled

Ronnie Problem?
Angie The heat.
Ronnie Angie, he's here. Mal's here.
Angie (*wearily*) Wheel him in, then. (*She shouts to Jo*) Keep going, Jo.
Ronnie Angie, be nice to him now. Be nice.

Ronnie goes out through her room

Angie (*after him*) Only if he's nice to me, I will be. (*She calls*) All right, Jo. Jo?

Jo enters, gasping for breath

Jo (*weakly*) Yes.
Angie You get two minutes rest, all right? (*She picks up the stopwatch*) Starting from—now.

Jo collapses on the ground

In one minute forty-four seconds, forty-three ... forty-two ... you start doing the exercises, all right? The ones I showed you. (*Muttering*) Tried to show you. All right?

Jo nods miserably

And, Jo—if I see you not doing them properly, you'll do them again. That body's in perfect nick. So it's mind over matter, girl.

Jo (*muttering*) There's nothing wrong with my mind.
Angie And shut up and save your breath or I won't eat your Mars bar. Seventy seconds left.

Ronnie comes out, followed by Mal. Mal is very subdued in manner and appearance. Actually, he looks half dead

Ronnie Here he is… The lad himself. Here she is, Mal. There you both are. There we be.

Pause

I'll go for a walk. Leave you both to it. All right?

Ronnie walks off down the garden

(*As he passes Jo*) Keep it going. Don't lose heart then.

Jo glares at him

Ronnie goes off down the garden

Mal 'llo, Ange.
Angie 'llo, Mal.
Mal Well.
Angie What a carry on, eh?
Mal Yes. How's the head?
Angie Oh, fine. Back on. You know.
Mal Yes.
Angie I hear you fell off the bandstand.
Mal Yes.
Angie You all right?
Mal Yes. (*He pauses*) I didn't fall. I jumped, really.
Angie Yes.
Mal I thought I'd—you know—killed you.
Angie Well, nearly.
Mal I didn't mean to do it. You know that.
Angie I know, I know you didn't really.
Mal I love you.
Angie I know. I know you do.
Mal Do you love me?
Angie Yes, I think I must do.
Mal Well, that's all right, then.

Angie Is it?

Mal Why shouldn't it be?

Angie (*yelling to Jo*) Fifteen seconds.

Mal What?

Angie I was talking to her.

Mal Oh. (*He stares at Jo*) Who's that, then?

Angie That's the other girl you... That was...

Mal Oh. She's the one who's got...?

Angie Yes.

Mal And you've got...?

Angie Yes. I thought you might have noticed.

Mal I did.

Angie I hope you did. (*She yells*) All right. Here we go. Stomach exercises for two minutes. On your back on the ground, legs up to ninety, down to forty-five, then open close, open close ... lower and start again. Starting— now. (*She clicks the watch again*) Right, where were we?

Mal is watching Jo, fascinated

(*Wearily*) This way, Mal. I'm over here. Remember?

Mal (*appreciatively*) Great.

Angie Are you listening?

Mal It is. That's definitely your body.

Angie (*alarmed*) Mal, you haven't mentioned this to anyone else, have you?

Mal Oh, no. Promise.

Angie Good. Now—Mal, would you mind looking at me while we're talking—we have things to discuss, you see, don't we?

Mal (*tearing himself away*) Oh, yes...

Angie Like the future of our marriage. Is it on or off?

Mal On. It's on. I thought we'd decided that.

Angie So it's agreed, is it?

Mal (*barely listening to her*) What?

Angie You're happy to accept things the way they are?

Mal Oh, yes.

Angie Mean it?

Mal Oh, yes.

Angie (*smiling*) Mal.

Mal (*smiling*) Angie.

Angie You know when you gave me that book—you remember—just before the accident...

Mal Oh, yes...

Angie I think that meant more to me than anything. It was the first thing you'd ever given me, Mal, that was—well, it was for me. To please me.

Everything before had been for your pleasure, hadn't it? Really? You know, see-through night-dresses and that. But that book, that was really just for me, wasn't it?

Mal Yes. Did you read it?

Angie No. I've had a lot on recently. But I'm very near to starting it.

Mal Only I think that was the wrong book.

Angie Was it?

Mal Jim told me the title but I checked with him and I think I wrote it down wrong. His was another book altogether. They said in the shop that was a very good book, though. They'd never heard of Jim's book.

Angie Oh, well, it doesn't matter. It's still a book, isn't it?

Mal I'll try and get you Jim's book as well.

Angie Goodness. Two books. Nearly have a library, then, won't I? (*She smiles at him*) I really want you, you know. I really do.

Mal Now?

Angie Oh, yes. Yes. Yes. Now.

During the following, Jo stops exercising and sits up and watches them

Mal (*sniffing*) What's the smell?

Angie Cologne, only cologne.

Mal Strong.

Angie Does it put you off?

Mal No, no...

Angie You thinking what I'm thinking, then?

Mal Probably.

Angie (*aware of Jo*) All right, Jo. Off you go. One more circuit round the trees.

Jo What are you...?

Angie Go!

Jo goes

(*Once Jo is gone*) Oh, Mal...

Angie kisses Mal deeply

Mal (*impressed by the strength of.Angie's response*) Bloody hell.

They kiss again. They finally part, rather breathless, both somewhat overcome

What happens now, then? What are we supposed to do?

Angie I'll ask her. I'll ask her permission——

Mal I see. Her permission to…? I see, to let us…

Angie …have it, yes.

Mal I see.

Angie It's mad. I want it like I've never wanted it in my life before, but I can't…

Mal Why not?

Angie Because—it's difficult to explain—this is still her body, you see— it's not my body, it's somebody else's. And I can't just—give it. Simply like that.

Mal You were happy enough to kiss me.

Angie Yes, well, that bit belongs to me. I can do what I like with that. She's got the rest of it. Look, I'll call you. If she's agreeable, I'll call you. OK?

Mal Couldn't you ask her now? It's quite urgent.

Angie No, I've got to do it properly. I can't just stick my head round the door and say, "Oy, Jo, can Mal have it away with your body, mate?" I have to ask her nicely. You must see that, Mal? Please.

Mal (*gloomily*) Right.

Angie I do want you so much. More than I've…

Mal Yes.

Angie Mal, come on. Don't get like that.

Mal No. Yes.

Angie I'll see you to the front door.

Mal Yes.

Angie goes into her room

Mal makes to follow but, as he does so, Jo returns from her lap round the trees

She throws herself down. Mal stops to stare at her

Angie returns for Mal

Mal… Come on.

Angie pulls Mal into her room

Jo sees this

Jo (*breathlessly*) What are they…? If she's having … if she's having it away … while I'm here doing… How's she managing to have it away, anyway? Looking like that? I never got it in five years. Five years… They are! I think they really are at it! How dare she! (*She is about to get up off the ground and investigate*)

Ronnie enters

Ronnie Hallo. Jacked it in, then, have you?

Jo Yes... Excuse me. I must get changed.

Ronnie (*confidentially*) Er... Listen. I wanted to say just one word. To put it crudely—excuse the bluntness... That body you have got, believe me, is an earner. That body has still got—what—maybe two, three good years left in it. You follow me? Now, if you wanted, you've got a pleasant face, it's not stunning, it won't stop traffic but it's not displeasing—I'm being honest here with you, you see, Jo, I know you'd want me to be honest, the point is if you fancy doing a little model work—I think I could fix it. Frankly, and I'm being absolutely frank, Jo, there is, yes—there is curiosity value attached as well, I won't deny it. But we won't push that too hard but it will be there, no doubt about that, why turn our backs on the facts, what do you say?

A silence. Jo stares at him incredulously

Jo You're asking me if I'd like to model.

Ronnie Absolutely.

Jo With this body?

Ronnie And that head. Don't forget the head, Jo. (*He laughs*) Mustn't forget that.

Jo No, I hadn't forgotten. I was thinking about the body. I mean, I know what the head thinks of your offer. I'm just not quite sure about the body.

Ronnie You're not?

Jo No. I'll have to consult its owner. May I give you an answer later?

Ronnie (*puzzled*) Of course, of course.

Jo Bye.

Ronnie Yes. (*He walks away*) See you later, then. (*He turns briefly, appreciatively*) Stunning.

Ronnie goes off along the lawn again

Jo, her anger now coming out, spies the Mars bar that Angie has left there. Impetuously, she picks it up and takes a large bite. Her face registers in swift succession first pleasure at the taste and then nausea as the unaccustomed substance reaches her protesting stomach

As this occurs, Angie comes into view in her room

Angie Jo, I'm sorry. I didn't mean to leave you like that. Could I ask you something urgent?

Jo (*angrily*) Are you going to eat this or aren't you?

Angie Sorry?

Jo This Mars bar. Do you intend to eat it or don't you?

Angie (*bewildered*) Yes. I was going to. I'm sorry. I hadn't forgotten. It's just I had an urgent——

Jo (*rather hysterically*) Then eat it! This is two way, you know. You might at least do something my body would actually enjoy, just for once!

Jo hurls the Mars bar down and stamps off to her room, furiously

Angie (*mystified*) Yes... (*Absent mindedly, she picks up the Mars bar and starts to gnaw at it rather suggestively but quite unselfconsciously. She realizes what she is doing*) Oh, what am I doing? (*She slaps her stomach and shouts*) Don't you ever get tired of eating, you—thing? (*She wipes her mouth*) It'll pull all my fillings out an' all. Fat woman with no teeth. Who's going to want me then?

Jo comes out of her room

Angie stares at her

Oh, hallo.

Jo sits moodily silent

Look, I'm sorry if I... I'm sorry.

Jo (*softly*) I can't live with it, Angie.

Angie What are you talking about?

Jo He has to get us back. He has to. This—body of yours. I can't cope with it.

Angie What's wrong with it, then?

Jo Oh, nothing. Nothing wrong. It's wonderful. It's perfect. Too perfect for me. It runs, it jumps, it can put both feet behind my ears——

Angie (*smiling wistfully*) You discovered that, did you...?

Jo It's other people I can't cope with. Women all look at me and hate me— I know they do—they're either jealous, or they think I'm a tart who's just helping to sell women short——

Angie Never. They don't think that. Well. Only a few of them.

Jo They all do, Angie. Underneath.

Angie Did you?

Jo Oh, yes. I hated you. I really hated you. Didn't you know?

Angie (*hurt*) Oh. No, I didn't. What about the men, then?

Jo The men—oh, don't talk about the men. If one more security man with acne propositions me in that canteen, I shall stick a fork up his nose. Haven't any of them got any dignity? Any pride, for God's sake? And now Ronnie's started...

Angie Ronnie? Ronnie propositioned you?

Jo Not in that way. He wants me to model. Not much of a face, but I've got a great little body...

Angie What did you tell him?

Jo I said I'd ask the owner. Angie, we have a deal. If you want me to model, I will model. I would find it extremely difficult but I will do it, I promise. If that's what you want...

Angie Do you want to?

Jo That's beside the point. What I want is beside the point. We have a deal until we switch back.

Angie I want to know. Do you want to model?

Jo Of course I don't.

Angie Then don't. Really. Don't.

Jo Thank you. (*Gratefully*) Thank you.

Angie I've got something to ask you too, actually. When Mal was here we—well, we...

Jo (*brusquely*) Good. Yes. I don't need to hear. That's fine. Well done.

Angie No, no. We didn't, that's the point.

Jo You didn't?

Angie I couldn't. I said I couldn't without asking you first. After all, as you say, we have this ... you know, agreement.

Jo Oh. I see. Yes. That's very sweet of you. What can I say?

Angie Would it be all right for us? Would it?

Jo Well, I don't see how I can... You both want to—obviously, I take it?

Angie Oh, yes. Please.

Jo He's—is he nice—you know?

Angie Oh, yes.

Jo You know—considerate.

Angie Oh, yes. We'd be ever so careful with it.

Jo Good.

Angie He's gentle. He's not—rough, you know.

Jo No, well, fine.

Angie He's much more tender than he looks.

Jo Yes, great, super.

Slight embarrassed pause

(*With a laugh*) I hope he's not disappointed.

Angie Oh no, I don't think he will be, no. I'm sure he won't.

Pause

Er...

Jo Yes?

Angie If you don't mind my asking you... Is your...? Are you...? Well, are you always this randy? I mean, I seem to be feeling like it all the time lately. I wish you'd pass on one of them security guards. I could do with one. I mean, is this normal...?

Jo (*a little flustered*) Yes, yes, it does tend to... Sometimes, yes. It depends, of course, on the—on the—on your time...

Angie Time, yes.

Jo Not all the time. God, no...

Angie (*relieved to hear this*) No, good...

Jo I mean, I couldn't have survived. I mean, I was on my own for...

Angie Yes. Oh, dear. Tricky for you.

Jo Yes, well, you find ways round it, you know. Keep busy.

Angie Yes.

Jo Worst comes to the worst, there's good old DIY.

Angie Pardon.

Jo Do it yourself.

Angie Oh, yes.

Jo I mean, feel free, if you...

Angie Thank you. I'll try not to.

Pause

(*Laughing nervously*) Supposed to turn you blind, isn't it?

They laugh

Jo Yes.

Angie You get strong cycles then, do you?

Jo Tend to.

Angie Yes. I haven't really...

Jo No, well, once you get into the swing. I should have warned you. Sorry.

Angie No. Not to worry.

Jo Ten Disprin and a hot-water bottle, I've never found anything else that works as well.

Angie Right.

Jo You're all right, are you?

Angie Yes, I just sail through it. Like a little clock, that's me.

Jo Lucky.

Angie Yes. Born lucky. Till now anyway.

Jo You're not very—well, since we're on the subject—would you have described yourself as under-sexed?

Angie Well, I wouldn't have before. But well, now, looking back, I think I probably was, you know. I mean, assuming this, how I am now, is normal. Would you have described yourself as normal, would you?

Jo Fairly normal, I think. I never felt I wasn't... Do you feel it's over-sexed?

Angie Oh, no. I wasn't saying that. It's great, actually.

Jo Good. Well, have fun.

Angie Thank you.

Jo (*laughing again*) I could probably do with the rest.

Angie (*laughing too*) Yes. Well, I'll give him a call then. Fix it up.

Jo Yes, do. Let me know how it goes. I mean, not the lurid details, of course, just...

Angie Yes, I will. I promise. You can have the details too, if you like.

Jo I'll put some proper clothes on. Maybe you could lend me some till I——

Angie Honestly, wear what's comfortable for you. I don't care.

Jo No, I'm being childish. It's your body. It's a very beautiful one. You've looked after it and given it a lot of love and care. And it ought to be seen. And if it turns women green and makes men foam at the mouth, then sod the lot of them. (*She holds out her arms*)

Angie hugs her. They stay together for a second. Angie giggles

What?

Angie Funny hugging yourself, isn't it?

Jo You for me and me for you.

Angie Yeah! Sisters under the skin!

Jo Yeah!

They move to their respective doors

(*Smiling*) See you at lunchtime. If you're good, I'll get you a security man. (*She wiggles her hips*)

Angie (*growling*) Nah! Two!

As they both go indoors, the Lights change to denote the passing of time

Scene 3

The same. Evening. A few days later

The lights are on in the house. The terrace is also lit. Only the lawn is in real darkness

Benjamin is outside, looking at the stars

Freya appears on the lawn

Freya Benjamin…

Benjamin Ah, Freya. What can I do for you?

Freya You are still content that this operation will happen tomorrow?

Benjamin Well…

Freya Even though it will not work?

Benjamin Now, we don't know that…

Freya It is impossible to work. Tomorrow you will have two dead girls. You want this?

Benjamin That is only conjecture…

Freya Do they want this?

Benjamin They have both expressed a strong desire to be reunited with their own bodies. They have every trust in Hravic.

Freya Then they are deluded. What is more, Hravic is deluding them.

Benjamin Why? Why should he do that?

Freya Because he wants to operate. But since he has done this operation already, he will do another operation instead, I know him.

Benjamin What are you talking about?

Freya Listen. Hravic is a small boy still. He is a nosy boy. And like all nosy boys he takes things to pieces. Only like all small boys, many times he cannot put them together again. Or worse still, he tries to improve them. I tell you, Benjamin, the man is mad, he is dangerous, he should be forcibly held and strapped into a strong tight bag. Please!

Benjamin Freya, please. You're getting this a little out of proportion, you know.

Freya You want dead women?

Benjamin Sssh!

Freya They will be dead! Tomorrow they will be dead!

Benjamin Freya, I'm afraid I must disagree with you here. I am personally assisting Hravic with the operations tomorrow and if I felt for one second that there was any undue risk I would hardly involve myself—or indeed jeopardise the reputation of this clinic. You are just going to have to accept that.

Freya (*quietly*) Murder. It is murder. You will both of you be murderers.

Benjamin (*frostily*) I'm sorry. There's no point in continuing this conversation. We must beg to differ. I have a dinner to go to. Excuse me.

Benjamin goes off

Freya stands for a second as if summoning some inner resolve. She moves to the lawn and kneels in the darkness, clasping her hands together. Dramatically lit from the windows of the clinic, she looks a little as if she was appearing in a production of St Joan

Freya (*prayerfully*) Keet! Keet im sneetilt! Im har poontessgerscoot! [God! God save me! I entrust myself to you!]

Jo comes from her room. She is wearing one of Angie's more tasteful and restrained outfits. The result is nonetheless designed to show off the assets of her figure. She wears a ribbon round her neck

Jo (*seeing Freya, startled*) Freya? You all right?
Freya (*rising*) I am positive.
Jo You sure?
Freya (*indicating her body*) In my country we have a saying "Soom britt ester zaccrineet". Sometimes this altar is also for sacrifice…

Freya goes off resolutely

Jo (*mystified*) What?

Angie has appeared in her room. She, too, has got the balance right. She is wearing a wig. She looks very good, dressed for her evening with Mal. She is unsuccessfully trying to fasten her ribbon around her neck

Angie (*calling*) Jo…?
Jo (*calling*) Hallo?
Angie (*calling*) Could you give me a hand a minute?
Jo (*calling*) Coming. (*She starts to move inside*)

At that point, Angie comes out on to the terrace

Angie, you look lovely.
Angie (*indicating her ribbon*) Could you do this for me?
Jo Sure. (*She helps Angie with the ribbon*) Mmm. What's the perfume?
Angie It's about a gallon and a half of Ecstasy. I'm sweating like a pig.
Jo There. (*She steps back to look at Angie*) Good. It looks good with that.
Angie I'm in and out of that bloody toilet every twenty seconds as well. Were you always like this? It's appalling. When did you ever get any social life?
Jo Sorry.
Angie I'm so nervous. I mean, what if he… Look at me. It's only Mal. My own husband, for God's sake. Here I am terrified. Like a fourteen year old. No, I was never like this. Not even at fourteen. I was always … always…
Jo Sure of yourself.
Angie Yes. Right. Dead sure. So cool, you wouldn't believe. Nothing phased me. Now, I'm scared to death. I've never wanted anyone so much—and I've never felt so…

Jo You look lovely. Honestly. No swe—No panic.

Angie First time he kisses me this bloody wig'll fall off anyway.

Jo Are you certain you need it?

Angie I need all the help I can get. I wish to God I looked as good as you do. Look at you. You look amazing, just standing there. (*With a cry*) Oh, it's not fair...

Jo You'll get it back tomorrow. What's your problem?

Angie That's not certain, is it? No, so far as romance is concerned, tonight has to be the night for me. I won't get a second shot. I'll either be dead or back to no longer fancying it again.

Jo smiles

You seem dead calm about it. You think there'll be no problem, then? Us swapping back?

Jo He did it before, didn't he?

Angie Yes.

Jo And this time—conditions should be better.

Angie Yes.

In Angie's room, the phone rings. She jumps

Oh, God! That'll be him, that'll be him.

Jo All right! All right! Keep calm...

Angie I don't think I can face him...

The phone rings again

Jo Angie, just answer the phone.

Angie Oh, God.

Jo Angie... Answer the phone...

Angie (*in a blind panic*) I can't...

The phone rings

Jo Well, someone's got to answer it... (*She goes into Angie's room*)

Angie Tell him I'm not here. Tell him I've had a relapse...

Jo (*answering the phone*) Hallo ... yes, she's here...

Angie No, she's not...

Jo ...yes, she'll be right out...

Angie No, she won't...

Jo (*with a glance at Angie*) ...one of us will be right out... (*She hangs up*) Security ... one of us has to sign him in...

Angie Oooohhh...

Jo I'll sign him in... Angie, sit there and calm down... what's the matter with you? ... He wants you ... he's desperate for you ... he's already said as much, hasn't he?

Jo goes off

Angie sits and takes deep breaths

Angie God, I'm randy...

Freya appears. She has done a quick change out of her usual semi-uniform into an evening dress. Whilst quite becoming, one has the impression that it is regulation issue given out by some Eastern European government department—female, evening clothing, seduction for the purpose of. Freya seems a little less assured than normal

She sees Angie and clears her throat

(*Looking up and seeing her, surprised*) Oh.
Freya Hallo.
Angie Hallo. You look nice. Going out, are you?
Freya Wet? [What?]
Angie Going somewhere nice?
Freya Yes. I am dating.
Angie Dating?
Freya Yes.
Angie You got a date, you mean?
Freya Yes. Hot date.
Angie Great.
Freya You have maybe some perfume?
Angie Perfume? Gallons of it. You want to borrow some, then?
Freya Please. A woman must smell.
Angie Yes. Come in here, then. I'll give you some.
Freya Thank you.

They both go into Angie's room. Angie selects a scent spray

Angie (*spraying some on the back of her hand*) Here. Do you fancy that? (*She holds out her hand for Freya to smell*)

Freya sniffs suspiciously

Freya Yes... It is ... musty.

Angie Musky, yes… It's quite nice. Once it settles down. Here. That'll get him going. (*She hands Freya the spray*)

Freya Yes. (*She starts to spray it rather wildly about herself*)

Angie Careful! Careful! Only a little… You'll start a riot. (*She takes the spray from Freya*) Here. Let me. (*She starts to apply the scent to Freya*) Keep it subtle. Just a little dab here. See? And a little dab here. That's all you need.

Freya Yes, yes. You are an expert, of course.

Angie Yes. Retired expert. Ex-expert. There.

Freya I look all right?

Angie (*not totally convinced*) Yes. Very nice.

Freya The bosoms, they are correct.

Angie Yes. All present and correct, yes. Could I suggest…

Freya Yes?

Angie Here. Sit down.

Freya sits meekly

You just need a little help with your eyes. May I? (*She picks up a mascara brush*) They're lovely eyes, they just need picking out a bit.

Freya Yes, yes. So.

Angie (*applying mascara to Freya*) Open wide. Close. That's it. Just a touch. Not too much.

Freya I do not wish to look prostitutional.

Angie No, no. You won't do that, I promise.

Freya I do not wish to be a pie…

Angie A tart, no… There. That's all you need. (*She shows Freya the mirror*) See?

Freya Yes. This is good.

Angie Sexy.

Freya Yes. Sexy. (*She pouts a little*)

Angie Yes. I wouldn't do that too much. Makes you look like a chicken.

Freya (*puzzled*) Chicken?

Hravic arrives in the garden. He appears to have had a drink or two

Hravic (*calling*) Freya! Freya! Vess putt, Memmer Hrootpucker! Freya!

Freya Ah. My date. He is here.

Angie (*stunned*) Your date? That is your date?

Freya Yes. Very sexy.

Angie God help you. I thought I was desperate.

Freya goes out into the garden. She has adopted a semblance of Angie's former walk

Freya (*calling softly*) Hravic! Hravic!

Hravic stares at her

Hravic!

Angie watches the following exchange with astonishment

Hravic Jit? Brutt gool Freya? [Yes? Is that Freya?]
Freya Jit. Gool Freya. Eeen fiss har shrigger, Hravic. [Yes, it's Freya. I want to talk to you, Hravic.] Een'st broke, Hravic. Een fiss quittle bit har, een'st noot hrootpucker. [I'm sorry, Hravic. I want to prove to you I'm not a dyke.]
Hravic (*incredulously*) Wet?
Freya Een ip bit har quittser, Hravic. Og har uttst im. [I will prove it to you, Hravic. If you will allow me.]
Hravic Quittser? [Prove it?]
Freya Jit. [Yes.]
Hravic Grerb? [Now?]
Freya Jit. [Yes.]
Hravic Vess? [Where?]
Freya Hot. Hot int grerb. Funt u sprinklers. Jit? [Here. Here and now. Under the stars. Yes?]
Hravic (*moving with alacrity*) Jit, jit. Nord timmlt? [Yes, yes. You're not joking?]
Freya (*reproachfully*) Een nord timmlt. [I'm not joking.]
Hravic Vip kinst drooler moon teets? [We can make love many times?]
Freya Moon, moon teets. Sairer teets. [Many, many times. Twenty times.]

They start to move off

Hravic Loot teets... [Thirty times...]
Freya Hrammer teets... [A hundred times...]

Freya and Hravic go off

Angie My God... Oh!

Jo leads Mal on to the terrace

Angie darts back into her room as she hears them coming, lurking nervously during the following

Jo We're just out here.

Mal Right.
Jo Sit down.
Mal Thanks.
Jo Oh. I'll see if I can find her. (*She moves to Angie's door*) Angie? Angie?
Angie 'llo.
Jo He's here. Mal's here.
Angie Right.
Jo Well, come on out, then.
Angie Right.

Angie comes out from her room rather nervously, encouraged by Jo

Hallo.
Mal Hallo.
Angie Sorry, I was just——

An awkward pause

Well, don't I get a kiss then?
Mal Oh, yes. Sure. (*He gets up and kisses her awkwardly*) I didn't realize you were going to be here——
Angie What?
Jo Well, I'll be off. Leave you to it—have fun, both of you. See you tomorrow. (*She makes to move into her room*)
Mal Hey! Just a sec.
Jo What?
Mal (*indicating Angie*) Don't leave me with her.
Angie What?
Jo What?
Mal I'm with you. I'm supposed to be spending the evening with you, aren't I?
Angie No, you're not.
Jo No.
Mal Well, who am I spending the evening with?
Angie Me.
Mal You?
Angie Yes. Who do you think? Did you think you were going to doss down with her?
Mal 'Course.
Jo Oh, come on...
Angie You're married to me, you berk...
Mal Only your top bit. (*He indicates Jo*) I'm married to the rest of her.
Angie You're joking. You were seriously considering getting your leg over with her?

Mal Why not?

Angie Why not? I keep telling you, because you're married to me, that's why, you pillock.

Mal Yes, well, that's you over there, isn't it?

Angie No, it isn't. (*She points at her head*) This is me standing here. It's me here. Right?

Mal From where I'm standing you're over there.

Angie Well, I'm bloody not. This is the bit that matters, here. Not that bloody bit.

Mal Well, that was the bloody bit I fell in love with and that was the bloody bit I married you for. You can keep that bit. I don't want that bit.

Angie Oh, terrific, thank you very much. (*She is on the verge of crying*) Oh, God, I'm not going to cry, am I? Please, it's not going to cry on me as well, is it? (*She hits her body angrily*)

Jo Now listen, Mal, I don't know what you think you're trying to do here...

Mal Listen, I'm being perfectly reasonable, all I'm saying is, I want my wife, OK? With my body I thee wed, all right? Now what about it?

Jo (*calmly*) All right. OK. I'm sure that'll all be perfectly in order. Personally, I'd love to.

Mal Great.

Angie (*to Jo*) What are you playing at?

Jo (*to Mal*) Excuse me, Mal. Angie...?

Angie What?

Jo Would it be all right for me to give Mal the body? Is that OK with you?

Angie No, it bloody isn't OK with me.

Jo (*disappointedly, to Mal*) Oh, I am sorry.

Mal Eh?

Jo She's just said no. Sorry.

Mal What?

Jo Damn. I am disappointed. I could have just done with that, too. I really felt like it. Damn, damn, damn. Never mind. I'll have a bath instead.

Mal Just a minute. Are you denying me access to my wife's body, is that it?

Jo No. She's denying you. I'm not. I'd love to accommodate you.

Mal (*moving a little towards Jo*) Now listen, you...

Jo You lay a finger on me and she'll scream the place down. Won't you?

Angie I will.

Mal Oh, very funny. Both of you. Very funny. All right. (*He turns to Angie*) If that's the way you want it to be, it'll have to be you then, won't it?

Angie (*brightening*) Oh, great. Wonderful. Thank you so much, Mal. I'm ever so grateful. That's OK, is it? Jo. Still all right for the loan of the body?

Jo Oh, Angie. Sorry. No.

Angie Oh?

Mal What?

Jo Sorry. It has this thing about being second choice, isn't that awful of it?

Angie No, not at all. Quite understood. Pity, I was really feeling like it too, what a shame... Sorry, Mal.

Mal (*moving to Angie*) Now wait a minute...

Jo You touch her, I'll scream the place down.

Mal looks confused

Mal All right. Big joke. What happens now?

Jo I think you go home, Mal, actually.

Mal Home?

Angie You've just blown your chances with two women in two minutes, lover. That must be a record even for you.

Mal Look, I was only...

Angie Go home, Mal. We don't want you. Any part of either of us. Piss off.

Mal I'm... It was just... I was... Yes, well, I... You see, I... Nothing to...

Pause

Yes, OK. (*He moves to the door. He stops and takes a package from his pocket*) I brought you that book anyway. See?

Mal puts the book on the table and goes out through Angie's room

A silence. Angie stares at the book

Angie That was considerate of him. Bringing me something to read whilst the rest of me was having a good time next door.

Jo Angie, I'm sorry. It's this bloody body. It does things to people.

Angie Yes, I know it does. Always has done. It's all right, I know it's not your fault. You know how some photographer described my bum once? We were doing this session, he called it the base that raunched a thousand shits—clever that, wasn't it? (*Tearfully*) It's just so bloody disappointing though, isn't it? When people turn out just what you expect them to be. Just for once, just bloody once, wouldn't it be great if someone turned out a lovely big surprise? Just once. (*She cries openly now*)

Jo comforts her

Jo Not everyone surely, Angie. Not everyone's a disappointment?

Angie (*muffled, angrily*) Name one. Name one who isn't.

Jo Well... I don't know. Am I a disappointment?

Angie You?

Jo Have you been disappointed in me? Perhaps you have.

Angie No. Not you. 'Course not.

Jo Well, there you are. One, then.

Angie Yes. I suppose. (*She stops crying a little*)

Jo All right?

Angie Yes. You got a...?

Jo (*finding her a tissue*) Here...

Angie Do you know, that's something else that's happened. Since I've been like this... I've started crying a lot, too. Every time I turn the telly on I cry. I even cry at commercials these days.

Jo (*laughing*) Really?

Angie Great big sentimental lump this is... Call yourself an intellectual?

Jo No, I never called myself an intellectual.

Angie Educated, though...

Jo Oh, yes. Educated. But the more educated you are, the more things you find to cry about...

Angie Stupid bastard. I should never have let him back, anyway. He's as stupid as hell and his band's lousy an' all. The only thing he ever did for me was cut my head off... Good riddance. I'm glad he didn't want me, so there.

Jo He may want you tomorrow.

Angie Why?

Jo When you get it all back.

Angie He may want me. He's not getting it. Ever.

As they stand musing on this, Hravic appears. He walks uncertainly. A man in the last throes. He sees the women

Jo (*seeing him*) What the...?

Hravic (*trying to speak, gasping for air*) Hroot... Hroot...

Angie What's he saying?

Hravic Hroot... Hrootpucker! (*With an angelic smile*) Benshter—geeeeeel! (*He falls forward and lies still*)

The two women stand stunned

Jo Oh, my God...

Freya appears. She looks slightly tousled

She bends over Hravic's body and examines it

Angie What's the matter with him?

Jo Is it serious?

Angie How is he?
Freya He is dead. I have been too much.
Jo Too much?'
Freya I fear I have over-sexed him...
Jo Oh, God.
Freya I must fetch someone. Excuse me. (*To Angie, as she goes*) It is your
perfume. It is this perfume that has done it...

Freya goes

A pause. Angie and Jo look at each other

Angie Well.
Jo Well.
Angie That's that then, isn't it?
Jo Yes.
Angie Stuck like this for ever.
Jo Permanently.
Angie Whether we like it or not.
Jo Yes.

Pause

Angie (*in a small voice*) Bloody hell.

*As they both move slowly to their respective rooms, the Lights change again
to denote the passing of time*

Scene 4

The same. It is morning. The good weather has gone

*The terrace itself is deserted but within the two rooms there appears to be a
lot of activity. Nurses are to-ing and fro-ing in both rooms, apparently
stripping the beds*

*In Angie's room, Ronnie is apparently helping her pack. In Jo's room, Derek
is also lending a hand. Neither woman is immediately visible*

A nurse appears in Jo's room and will exit during the following

Ronnie (*appearing with a suitcase*) I'll move this out of your way, nurse. I'll move it out of your way. (*He dumps the suitcase down*) I ask you, nurse, have you ever known man or woman come to hospital with so many suitcases? You'd think this was a hotel. Right? I bet you'll be glad to see the last of her, eh? No, no, I'll move that one too. Don't you do that. It's heavy, my dear. It's very heavy.

Ronnie moves off

The nurse has gone from Jo's room

Derek appears at the window. He has his camera

He squints through the viewfinder at the view outside

Derek Very dark. Not much light. Still pissing down out here. (*He holds up his light meter*) I don't think it's going to clear either. I'll have to get you both out here... You can have a brolly. Only for a second. I'll need some of you both together, won't I?

Angie appears and stands gloomily at her window. She is dressed to leave. She has on a mac and a beret over her wig

Angie Still raining. It's horrible out here. I've just had a look. They're all outside the gates there. Waiting for us. The whole rat pack.
Derek Look, you're not going to be back here, are you? If I don't do it now, I'm going to miss my exclusive, aren't I?

As Derek disappears from view, Ronnie appears with an armload of bits and pieces of Angie's. Sponge bags, slippers, etc.

Ronnie I'm now your official packer, as well as everything?
Angie You're my manager. You pack.
Ronnie Yes, and as your dogsbody manager, may I be so bold to ask, Angie, if you've yet come up with a decision? These people are waiting.

Ronnie disappears, momentarily

Angie I gave you my decision last night. It was no then, it's no now. Nude is still nude, isn't it?

Ronnie reappears with his bundle

Ronnie Medically nude. They have dozens of books filled with them. Straightforward body shots, strictly for medical interest only.

Angie Yes, I can see all those doctors in their macs now, crowding round the book stalls...

Ronnie Do you realize how much they'll pay for one picture?

Angie That's final, Ronnie. I'm not having this body turned into a freak show. Not this one.

Ronnie Great crowd out there. The publicity, Angie, it's going to be fantastic. (*He comes across the book that Mal brought. It is still in a bag on the table*) What about this? Do you want this?

Angie What is it?

Ronnie I don't know. It's a book.

Angie Oh yes, Mal brought it for me.

Ronnie (*removing it from the bag and reading the cover*) Punishment *Without Crime*. A short history of flagellation and bondage from Roman times to the present day. Fully illustrated. You want me to pack it?

Angie No, I don't want you to pack it, thank you, Ronnie. I'll carry on reading the other one.

Ronnie What shall I do with it?

Angie Eat it.

Ronnie (*putting it back on the table*) I'll leave it for the nurses.

Angie Yes, they'll love it, you do that.

Jo has appeared now. She is similarly dressed in hat and coat for the journey

She stands at her window. She seems as downcast as Angie

Ronnie (*looking to the door*) Ah-ha. Here he is, Mr Ben. The man himself come to say goodbye. Angie, Benjamin has come to say goodbye.

Angie Oh, yes. Good-morning. (*She turns from the window*)

Benjamin steps into view

Ronnie goes

Benjamin ...Just to say once again, Angie, how sad we all are that—things have worked out quite as they have.

Angie Make the best of it, then, mustn't we?

Ronnie appears in view

Ronnie Angie, I'm going to start putting the cases in the car, all right?

Ronnie disappears again

Benjamin Obviously, from the clinic's point of view, most of the publicity is highly unwelcome. It does tend to reflect us in a rather—shall we say, ill-organised light—and for you, of course, it will mean a lot of unnecessary and painful media scrutiny.

Angie It's all right. I'm used to painful media scrutiny.

Derek appears again in the other room

Derek Jo, come on. You promised me my exclusive…

Jo (*off*) Wait! You'll get your exclusive.

Benjamin On the brighter side, though, all of us here have gained a very valuable colleague in Freya Roope. I, for one, am personally very much looking forward to working alongside her. (*He moves to pick up Mal's book*)

Derek moves away from the window and disappears

What's this? Is it a good read?

Angie Oh, it was something that got left here. I haven't read it.

Benjamin (*flipping the pages*) Oh, yes, it looks rather intriguing.

Angie Take it. Be my guest.

Benjamin Well, I might, when I've a… (*He gesticulates*) Thank you. (*He tucks the book in his pocket*) Well, no point in prolonging things further. I've said goodbye to—to Jo. So. Angie, this is goodbye and good luck.

Angie Goodbye, Benjamin. And thank you for everything.

They shake hands

Benjamin And as I usually say to patients when they leave here—I sincerely hope we won't see you again. (*He smiles at his own tired joke*) Goodbye.

Benjamin leaves

In Jo's room, Derek reappears with an umbrella

He steps out on to the terrace. He makes his way to the steps, sheltering his camera from the rain. He waves at Angie, who stands watching him

Derek (*waving to her*) Come on! Come on, then!

Angie What?

Derek Outside!

Angie You're joking, in this?

Jo appears in Angie's room. She is also carrying an umbrella

Jo He wants a quick shot of us, would you mind? I promised him an exclusive before the rest of them are let loose. Would you mind?

Angie Oh, yes? Sure he wants me?

Jo Of course he does. Both of us. I've brought a brolly. Come on.

Jo leads her outside, opening the umbrella

You've got two minutes, Derek. That's all.

Derek Bless you, girls. Thanks. Could you get very close together? Under the umbrella. That's it. Tilt it back from your faces. I need the light. Lovely. Could you put your heads together? Cheek to cheek, that's it. That's lovely, that's really beautiful.

Angie We're going to get so sick of all this, you know.

Derek You're so beautiful, you've no idea. Big smiles, girls, come on. Come on, Jo, smile.

Jo *(through pursed lips)* I am smiling.

Angie It's bloody cold out here, Derek.

Derek Right, perfect. Jo, could I just get a couple of you on your own. Separately. Do you mind, Angie?

Angie No. *(She stands aside)*

Derek Take the umbrella from Jo, would you?

Jo hands Angie the umbrella

Jo I'm going to get soaked.

Derek Two seconds. Just natural. That's lovely, one there.

Angie Once we're outside these gates it's going to be hell on wheels. They're all out there waiting.

Derek That's beautiful, one just there. Give me that smile, Jo.

Angie Have you seen them? They'll be swarming all over us for ever. Ronnie's already sorting out the highest bidder.

Derek Give me that personality. Lovely. Beautiful. Now, unbutton the coat a bit, Jo. Just a couple of buttons.

Jo Derek! It's pissing with rain...

Derek Come on, come on...

Jo, a little unused to this, starts to unbutton

Jo *(as she does this, to Angie)* Why sell?

Angie How do you mean?

Jo It's our story, isn't it?

Angie *(looking at her)* You mean...?

Jo Write it ourselves. *(She has her coat off and has resumed posing)*

Derek That's it. That's better.

Jo At least that way we can say it like we want it said. Why not? After all, I am a journalist. If you're agreeable, that is?

Derek (*as he continues snapping*) Tell you what. Just slip the coat off altogether. Just for a minute. Angie, hold the coat for Jo. There's a good girl.

Jo Derek, what are you doing?

Derek Come on, Jo...

Jo No...

Derek Ten seconds... You promised me...

Jo I never promised you this— (*She takes off the coat*) Oh, here...

Angie Fifty-fifty? We write it together and go fifty-fifty?

Jo 'Course. (*She smiles*) With your brains and my body, Ange...

Angie Worth a bit, eh?

Jo (*handing her coat to Angie*) Angie, if we play our cards right, a fortune.

Derek That's it. Now walk, walk for me, Jo baby.

Jo Walk?

Derek Come on towards me... Come on...

Jo (*stopping, looking at Angie, suddenly aware of what she's doing*) What am I doing? What the hell am I doing here?

Angie (*shrugging, not unamused*) Don't look at me. I'm only the bag lady.

Jo (*to Derek*) Oh, get stuffed, Derek... (*She snatches her coat back from Angie and starts to put it on again*)

Derek What you doing?

Jo Get lost.

Derek What do you mean? I need the picture. I haven't got the picture.

Jo You've got the picture. It's me and her together. That's the picture, Derek.

Derek No, I need——

Jo The only picture.

Angie (*blowing a kiss to him*) Piss off, sweetheart. It's national fat lady week.

Derek (*bewildered*) What's going on?

From now on they both ignore him

Jo Oh, we mustn't forget the other thing...

Angie What?

Jo Repeat after me... I hereby hand over—remember, we were going to do it officially?

Angie Oh, yes, like this, then...

They stand facing each other and hold up one hand apiece and press the palms together

Jo I hereby hand over...

Angie I hereby hand over...

Derek What are you doing?

Jo (*to Angie*) ...hand over my body...

Angie ...hand over my body...

Jo ...to Angie...

Angie ...to Jo...

Jo ...on the understanding that...

Angie ...on the understanding that...

Derek (*offering his own umbrella*) Want this one, as well?

Angie (*taking it*) Yes, go away, we're busy.

Jo ...that she may hereon treat it according to her own personal wishes and whims...

Angie ...that she may hereon treat it according to her own personal wishes and whims...

Derek ...both gone nuts if you ask me... I'd have had that on every front page.

Derek goes into Jo's room and disappears out of sight

Jo ...without fear of recrimination from its previous owner...

Angie ...without fear of recrimination from its previous owner...

Jo ...and may she live a prosperous, happy and fulfilled life in her new body...

Angie ...and may she live a prosperous, happy and fulfilled life in her new body...

Jo ...for so long as she may occupy it.

Angie ...for so long as she may occupy it.

Jo That's it.

Angie No. So help me God.

Jo So help me God.

Pause

Goodbye, body. (*She gives a little wave at Angie's*)

Angie (*doing the same to Jo's*) Bye.

Another slight pause

(*With sudden urgency*) Right, enough of that. Come here, new body. I've got one or two matters to sort out with you.

Angie collapses her umbrella and tosses it through the doorway into her room. During the next, she starts to take off her coat. Jo watches her with some surprise

Could we afford a yacht, do you think?

Jo Yes, why not? What's happening?

Angie A big one?

Jo Huge. What are you doing?

Angie Go round the world then, couldn't we?

Jo Easily. What are you doing, you'll get soaked?

Angie Can we afford a Roller an' all?

Under her coat, Angie is wearing a loose tracksuit. She now takes off her hat and wig in one and tosses these aside, too

Jo Two of them. Hers and hers. Have you've gone mad?

Angie I need to exercise. I have to lose weight now. This instant. I can't stay like this a minute longer, I'm sorry.

Jo It's pouring.

Angie It's all right, Jo. You don't have to bother. You can sit in the dry now all day long and eat chocolate. You don't ever need to exercise ever again… (*She runs down on to the lawn*)

Jo (*suddenly*) Hang on, Angie, I'll help you. I'll get the watch.

Angie No need.

Jo Where is it?

Angie In my bag, just in there.

Jo One sec…

During the following, Jo discards her own coat and hat in Angie's room. We see she is also wearing some form of tracksuit

Angie Don't if you don't want to. Oo! Ow! (*She jumps up and down on the lawn, starting to do the arm and leg scissor exercises. She finds it tough going*) God, this is killing me. I used to be able to do this for hours…

Jo looks in Angie's bag for the watch. She finds it. Something else in there also catches her eye

Jo, come on.

Jo Right. (*She removes a chocolate bar, takes a swift glance in Angie's direction, has a bite and stuffs the rest of it into her pocket rather guiltily*)

Angie (*breathlessly*) What you doing?

Jo Here I come. (*She comes out and sits on the edge of the terrace, the watch in her hand*)

Angie continues doing the scissors

Come on, hup—hup—hup... You can do better than that, girl... Two minutes from—now.

Angie It's all right for you, sitting there...

Jo Come on, mind over matter. Hup—hup—hup—hup... (*She takes another sly bite of chocolate*)

Angie (*suspiciously*) What are you eating?

Jo Nothing. One and two...

Angie Yes, you are. Your mouth's stuffed with chocolate.

Jo No, it's not. Hup and two...

Angie You've been at my choccy bar...

Jo Want a bit?

Angie No...

Jo Then keep going then. Thirty seconds.

Angie Bloody Mars bars, I ask you. Where's the justice? Where's the justice in it?

Jo ...Twenty ... nineteen ... eighteen ... seventeen... Oh, I've dreamt of this. I've dreamt of it. How did I live without chocolate? Ten ... nine ... eight ... seven...

Angie I warn you, I put on weight very, very easily... You'll be twenty stone before you know it...

Jo (*eating happily*) Too bad. Too bad...

Jo continues to direct Angie's exercise programme, happily gnawing at her chocolate bar. Despite Angie's complainings, both women seem happier than we've ever seen them. The rain is now louder and drowns their voices though we can see them still laughing and talking. In due course, Jo lays aside the half eaten chocolate bar and, jumping up, joins Angie with her exercises, encouraging her and working alongside her. Angie stops momentarily and, leaving Jo exercising on her own for a moment, has a quick bite of the chocolate bar herself. As the two women exercise and picnic in the rain, a Light and sound freeze on the two which captures them briefly in motionless, silent joy

Black-out

FURNITURE AND PROPERTY LIST

Further dressing may be added at the director's discretion

ACT I

Scene 1

On stage: Small writing table
Chair
Stone steps with wooden ramp
Desk. *On it*: sun-glasses

Off stage: Two sticks (**Hravic**)
Rug, **Hravic**'s notebooks, writing materials (**Freya**)
Rug, cushion (**Nurse**)
Blanket (**Nurse**)
Large shoulder bag containing Mars bar, portable tape recorder,
    microphone (**Jo**)
Folded sheet (**Nurse**)
Mobile phone (**Ronnie**)
Book in gift-wrapped box (**Mal**)

Personal: **Hravic:** panama hat
Derek: camera, light meter

Scene 2

On stage: As before

Off stage: Clipboard (**Benjamin**)
Bowls, dressings, medical paraphernalia (**Nurses**)

Personal: **Jo:** tight-fitting cap, bandages
Angie: tight-fitting cap, bandages

ACT II

Scene 1

On stage: As before

Off stage: **Angie** and **Jo** in wheelchairs (**Nurses**)
               Vast bunch of flowers (**Ronnie**)

Personal: **Jo:** bandages, woollen hat, blanket
               Angie: bandages, woollen hat, blanket

Scene 2

On stage: As before

Off stage: Stopwatch, bag containing Mars bar (**Angie**)

Scene 3

Set: Scent spray
               Mascara brush

Personal: **Angie:** wig
               Mal: book
               Jo: tissues

Scene 4

On stage: Suitcase
               Angie's sponge bags
               Angie's slippers
               Bag containing **Mal**'s book and Mars bar

Off stage: Umbrella (**Derek**)
               Umbrella (**Jo**)

Personal: **Derek:** camera, light meter
               Angie: mac, wig, beret
               Jo: hat, coat

LIGHTING PLOT

Property fittings required: nil
1 mixed setting. The same throughout

ACT I, Scene 1

To open: Sunny June morning lighting

Cue 1   **Ronnie** rushes back into the house   (Page 36)
            Change lights to denote passing of time

ACT I, Scene 2

To open: Duller summer morning lighting

Cue 2   **Jo** and **Angie** slowly lift their robes   (Page 41)
            Fade lights to spots on women's faces

Cue 3   **Angie** and **Jo**: "Uuurrrrrg!"   (Page 41)
            Black-out

ACT II, Scene 1

To open: Bright summer morning lighting

Cue 4   **Jo** and **Angie** shudder as they touch   (Page 52)
            Change lights to denote passing of time

ACT II, Scene 2

To open: Summer morning lighting

Cue 5   **Jo** and **Angie** go indoors   (Page 65)
            Change lights to denote passing of time

ACT II, Scene 3

To open: Lights on in house and on terrace

Cue 6   **Jo** and **Angie** move slowly to their rooms   (Page 76)
               Change lights to denote passing of time

ACT II, Scene 4

To open: Rainy morning lighting

Cue 7   **Jo** and **Angie** exercise and picnic   (Page 84)
               Spot on **Jo** *and* **Angie***, then black-out*

EFFECTS PLOT

ACT I

Cue 1   To open Scene 1   (Page 1)
                 Birds singing

Cue 2   **Derek** starts to photograph helicopter   (Page 29)
                 Sound of helicopter engines growing loud; increasing
                 slipstream effect

Cue 3   **Jo** clutches her notes   (Page 30)
                 Helicopter landing sounds, sound of rotors slowing
                 down; slipstream fading

Cue 4   **Angie**: "Brilliant."   (Page 35)
                 Sound of helicopter being started

Cue 5   **Angie**: "Mal!"   (Page 35)
                 Sound of helicopter engine revving, slipstream

Cue 6   **Mal**'s awful cry is heard   (Page 35)
                 Sound of helicopter engines gradually stopping

ACT II

Cue 7   To open Scene 1   (Page 42)
                 Birds singing

Cue 8   **Angie**: "Yes."   (Page 68)
                 Phone rings in **Angie***'s room*

Cue 9   **Angie**: "I don't think I can face him…"   (Page 68)
                 Phone rings

Cue 10   **Angie**: "I can't…"   (Page 68)
                 Phone rings

Cue 11   To open Scene 4   (Page 76)
              Rain sounds and effect

Cue 12   **Jo** and **Angie** continue to exercise and picnic   (Page 84)
              Rain sounds louder, to freeze at end